DATE DUE

Accountability for Teachers and School Administrators

Accountability for Teachers and School Administrators

READINGS IN CONTEMPORARY EDUCATION

Edited by

ALLAN C. ORNSTEIN
Department of Education
Loyola University of Chicago

FEARON PUBLISHERS

Lear Siegler, Inc., Education Division • Belmont, California

To FRANCINE and RICKY
*Geographical distance separates us, but family
bonds unite us.*

ISBN-O-8224-0055-3

Library of Congress Catalog Card Number: 72-95012.

Printed in the United States of America.

Contents

Preface

Accountability for Teachers and School Administrators focuses on one of the major trends in education. The concept of accountability is borrowed from the field of business management, and when it is applied to education it means to hold some people (teachers or school administrators), some agency (board of education or state department of education), or some organization (professional group or private company) responsible for performing according to some agreed-upon terms. In the past, only the students were held accountable for their performance in school. Now, the finger is beginning to point in other directions, and the concept of accountability is taking on different forms and its advocates are growing in numbers.

One of these forms is the idea of making teachers and school administrators accountable for the realization of specific objectives relating to changes in students' achievement and behavior. In traditional methods of rating teachers, evaluation of classroom performance is an end in itself, but the subjective methods used in those evaluations have proven grossly inadequate. The process of rating school administrators has often been even more faulty—sometimes tainted with politics or else weighted with norms and rules that overemphasize the *status quo*. Today, in most accountability plans, the effects of the actions of teachers and school administrators on students' performances are measured not just by academic achievement tests, but also by criterion-referenced tests that measure a number of specified objectives.

There is also a growing trend toward the use of performance contracting. In this plan, a private firm (or group of professionals) contracts to teach reading, mathematics, or other subjects with the provision that the contracting agency will be paid a specified amount dependent upon and relating to specific gains achieved by the students within a given time period. For example, a contract might stipulate that the school system will pay the company $100 for each student who makes a one-year gain in reading within six months and $150 for each student who makes the same reading gain in four months.

The first performance contract, between the Texarkana, Arkansas, school system and Dorsett Educational Systems, was entered into in October 1969. The final evaluation of that program by Dean C. Andrew and Lawrence H. Roberts, was critical of the gains purported to have been achieved. They charged that the company had programmed into the learning machines as much as 60 percent of the questions appearing on the existing tests. Since the Texarkana experiment, however, over 250 performance contracts have been signed between school boards and private companies.

Most people probably believe that everyone, including teachers and school administrators, should be held accountable for their work. The problem comes in transforming this desire into a workable policy. How do we answer the charge "That's all good in theory, but it doesn't work in practice"? How do we transform generalities into specifics? How do we replace the rhetoric with reason? This book explores some of these questions. Other related problems are considered and some improvements in accountability procedures are proposed. Included are the writings of many of the most prominent educators and researchers at work in this field. Together the articles produce a balanced picture of the controversy surrounding accountability.

The book is divided into six parts: (1) The Concept of Accountability, (2) Accountability and the Teaching Profession, (3) Accountability Proposals and Methods, (4) Performance Contracting, (5) Limitations of Accountability Tests and Measurements, and (6) Extending the Boundaries of Accountability. In selecting articles, the editor has attempted to present a broad range of views on the subject. In addition, he tried to select articles that would give the reader some perspective on the larger dimensions of the problems and prospects and would raise pertinent questions that would lead to further discussion.

Naturally, my own views on the issues involved had some impact on the selection of articles and organization of the book. No matter how hard he tries, no editor of an anthology can escape from his own biases. All he can do is to state his views on the subject and let the reader make the final judgment. My views are that accountability has now reached bandwagon status, and that we should temper our enthusiasm with moderation.

The book is intended primarily for pre-service and in-service teachers and school administrators. However, the functions and problems of education now concern increasingly larger segments of our society, and this book should enjoy a wide audience among all those interested in the future of our schools.

Allan C. Ornstein

1

The Concept of Accountability

The management of a business firm is charged with organizing the company's resources, employees, and capital into an efficient and successful operation. Although the purposes of a public institution differ from the profit goal of private institutions, many schools are beginning to apply management techniques and policies developed by industry to the process of education. The growing use of accountability plans is one reflection of this trend.

The book begins with an article by Leon M. Lessinger, who defines accountability and explains the reasons behind its growing influence. He contends that schools are in serious condition—plagued by increasing costs, declining student achievement, and an erosion of public confidence. The accountability concept, according to Lessinger, revitalizes a school's commitment to student learning; fosters innovation, experimentation, and technological development; and introduces management policies based on cost effectiveness, demonstrated modes of proof, and systems design techniques. This concentration on management techniques, he points out, shifts the focus of the school's attention from its input to its output.

The Powerful Notion of Accountability in Education

Leon M. Lessinger

Accountability is a policy declaration adopted by a legal body such as a board of education or a state legislature requiring regular outside reports of dollars spent to achieve results. The concept rests on three fundamental bases: *student accomplishment, independent review* of student accomplishment, and a *public report,* relating dollars spent to student accomplishment. The grand jury, the congressional hearing, the fiscal audit are powerful and well-tested examples of means for achieving accountability. The absolute requirement of independent replication and communication in establishing scientific phenomena is another example of accountability. Accountability in education shares substance from all these examples. By focusing upon results, on student achievement, it can be a most powerful catalyst in achieving that basic reform and renewal so sorely needed in the school system.

A growing number of influential people are becoming convinced that it is possible to hold the schools—as other important agencies in the public and private sector are held—to account for the results of their activity. In his March [1970] Education Message, President Nixon stated, "From these considerations we derive another new concept: *Accountability.* School Administrators and school teachers alike are responsible for their performance, and it is in their interest as well as in the interest of their pupils that they be held accountable."

The preamble to the agreement between the Board of Education of the City of New York and the United Federation of Teachers for the period of Sept. 8, 1969, through Sept. 8, 1972, under the title Accountability says:

> The Board of Education and the Union recognize that the major problem of our school system is the failure to educate *all* our students and the massive academic retardation which exists especially among minority group students. The Board and the Union therefore agree to join in an effort, in cooperation with universities, community school boards and parent organizations, to seek solutions to this major problem and to develop objective criteria of professional accountability.

Dr. Lessinger is former Associate U.S. Commissioner of Education and is now Dean of Education at the University of South Carolina. This article originally appeared in the *Journal of Secondary Education* (December 1970). Copyright © 1970 by California Association of Secondary School Administrators. Reprinted by permission.

Many more pronouncements, program developments, and policy decisions of a similar sort could be described. A few examples follow:

1. The Oregon State Department of Education has employed a Director of Education Audits and is using an institute of educational engineering to promote its research and development activities.
2. The Virginia State Board of Education has encouraged and authorized the use of Title I ESEA funds (with USOE stimulation) for performance contracting with private enterprise to eliminate deficits in reading and other academic skills among disadvantaged children in Virginia.
3. The guidelines for the federal bilingual and drop-out prevention program require an independent educational accomplishment audit.
4. The Louisville, Kentucky, school system has an assistant superintendent for accountability.
5. The Colorado Legislature is considering the adoption of an accountability program.
6. The Office of Economic Opportunity is funding twenty-one school centers to experiment with performance contracts and incentives to achieve accountability.
7. The Dallas, Texas, school system is developing a "second generation" Texarkana project to eliminate basic school failure among its disadvantaged children through performance contracts to be checked by an outside audit.
8. The Florida State Legislature has appropriated $1.2 million to establish accountability through development of a variety of student output measures and other programs.
9. The Commission of the States has declared that its central theme along with National Assessment for the 1970's is accountability.
10. The President of the National School Boards Association has made accountability the theme of his administration.

The list could be extended to fill the entire presentation. Clearly a new educational movement is under way. The school systems of America are entering what the Washington Post has termed "An Age of Accountability."

Many of the early school laws in America called for accountability. The concept has been rediscovered and elaborated to meet serious conditions in the schools especially those conditions relating to galloping costs, poor student achievement, and the erosion of public authority and confidence in the schools.

Accountability's pointed thrust for a regular public report of an outside review of demonstrated student achievement promise for the allocation of resources will fundamentally alter public education. Some of the more important changes are now discussed.

In the first place, successful implementation of an accountability policy will shift the principal focus in the school system from input to output, from teaching to learning. A growing research literature points up the independence of teaching and learning. There can be teaching without learning and learning without teaching. There can, of course, be learning as a result of teaching. So independent is this relationship, that some have called the phenomenon the "teaching/learning paradox." This suggests that the present and traditional methods of requesting resources as well as the principal bases for judging the quality of schools will undergo drastic change. In place of equating quality in terms of resources allocated in the form of inputs (e.g., teachers, space, equipment, etc.), the important criterion will be results—student learning. This will lead to a second by-product of accountability, a revised educational commitment for the nation.

In principle the American educational commitment has been that every child should have access to an adequate education—this is the familiar, but still unattained, principle of equal educational opportunity. This commitment has been translated into the dollar allocations for the people and the "things" of education. When a child has failed to learn, school personnel have often assigned him a label—"slow," or "unmotivated," or "retarded." Accountability triggers a revised commitment—that every child *shall* learn. Such a revision demands a "Can Do" spirit of enterprise, a willingness to change a system which does not work and find one which does; a seeking of causes of failure as often in the system, its personnel, its organization, its technology, and its knowledge base as is now spent in seeking it solely in students. This revised commitment may come to be called the principle of equity of results. The call for everyman's "Right To Read" clearly foreshadows this tradition.

A third major effect of accountability on schools centers on the technology of instruction and the notion of better standard practice in America's schoolrooms. Without accountability for results, the spread of good practice and the adoption of better technology has moved at a snail's pace. In this connection, it should be remembered that technology is more than equipment, though equipment may be a part of technology. Technology refers to validated practice—the use of tested means to secure demonstrated results. It is the essence of the meaning in the phrase, "what works."

From an organizational, managerial, and technological point of view, education is a cottage industry. It is in a backward state, passed by in a time of striking and exciting development in other significant areas of societal activity. As many educators can testify, educational technology is primitive. Teachers and students barely understand the breadth of use to which the household telephone can be used to gather knowledge. And while the telephone is being redesigned to operate in milliseconds under automated commands, education is just beginning to cope with the manual dial.

The example of the equipment portion of technology is not unique. The important part in validated practice played by professional competence in interpersonal behavior, is not used in many classrooms. There is a wealth of evidence acquired over the last thirty years about the ways in which people interact, learn from each other, intervene, aid, support, or undermine the work of each other. Yet, there are few teachers who have progressed beyond the classroom methods of several generations ago. In few other fields of any consequence are there patterns of behavior so predictable, so unchanged, so inefficient in terms of the contemporary human organism and how it learns as are commonly found in the classroom.

Accountability is the "hair shirt" of formal education. It is the response at budget time to the question, "What did you do with that other money?" It is contained in the cry of the outraged parent, "If you don't teach my child, I'm going to have you fired."

There is little to be gained by defensiveness or protestation on the part of educators. Nor is a ringing statement of the truly magnificent achievements of the public schools an effective antidote. Hand wringing or defensiveness is not the same as problem solving. Public institutions cannot run on the record of more of the same when conditions and public expectancies have changed. Accountability represents an attractive path for improving support and strengthening the schools. The process of implementing an accountability directive contains elements which can bring new capability and new insights to personnel. These elements are now discussed. The major elements treated here are: developmental capital, modes of proof, and education engineering. Built on these foundations, accountability can be welcomed by teachers and administrators—the evidence is accumulating that this is happening. Without them, the concept can be disruptive and even dangerous. There is a history of danger in movements that center on efficiency and effectiveness so ably discussed, for example, in Callahan's *Cult of Efficiency.*

Developmental Capital and Accountability

Money available in a predictable and secure manner for responsible investment enables management in both school personnel and private enterprise to produce results. This is the energy of accountability.

This is a fourth major aspect of accountability. Developmental capital is the money set aside for investment by school leaders in promising activities, suggested by teachers, students or whomever, which produce results. Added to a good base of solid support plus equalization, such monies can act as the "steering" mechanism and the "propeller" to move the "ship" ahead in the desired directions.

Business typically budgets amounts varying from 3 to 15 percent for improved products, service, sales, or capability. Until the passage of the Vocational Education Act of 1963 and the Elementary and Secondary Act of 1965, there was virtually no comparable money in education. With the passage of these acts and subsequent amendments, it is estimated that there is now approximately 1/3 of 1 percent available as developmental capital.

School people need funds around which to bid for the opportunity to show results. The investment of small amounts of venture capital, administered in ways that call out the maximum involvement by staff, together with an outside audit of delivery on the promises to perform has been shown to be very effective. Such an approach needs widespread adoption by states and local education agencies in addition to the federal partner.

School systems today are characterized by archaic budgeting systems; poor use of buildings, staff, and equipment; salaries unrelated to performance; inadequate personnel development programs; poorly developed promotion systems; outmoded organization; and often repetitious and uninspired instruction. Developmental capital can serve as the incentive to cause movement toward change. It can be the necessary energy to cause the adoption, installation, and successful long-term utilization of better practice and systemwide reform. The experience of the author as a superintendent of schools managing a 1 percent fiscal set-aside in conjunction with teacher hearings as the quality control is an instructive example.

Modes of Proof and Accountability

The "eye" of accountability lies in the phrase, "modes of proof." Recognition of an expanded notion of assessment of results is a fifth major effect of accountability on school reform. For too long, many have confused measurement of results in education with standardized achievement testing of the paper-and-pencil, normal curve-based variety. Not everything in education can be (or ought to be) quantified in such a manner. But accountability in education, like accountability in other governmental enterprises, can make use of "evidence" from a variety of modes of attaining evidence. The use of hearings, of experts, of certified auditors, of simulations of work situations, together with such means of acquiring evidence as video-tape and demonstrated pupil performance selected using small sample statistics, come easily to mind. To argue that scientific measurement is limited to narrow so-called objective tests is to display ignorance of the rich field of assessment, limited experience with science, and inability to foresee the rapid development of creative output instruments and strategies which money and attention can promote. The Eight-Year Study and the O.S.S. Assessment of Men activities certainly give cause for optimism in this regard.

The outside review component of accountability is the most vital mode of proof. Science relies for its very existence on qualified, independent review and replication. Nothing is established in science unless and until it can be demonstrated by someone other than he who claims discovery or invention. Scientists are neither better people nor better scholars than educators; they do not pursue more scientifically or intrinsically "better" problems than teachers. They are simply subject to better monitoring by a system that both encourages and mobilizes the criticism of competent peers throughout their lives. Education, on the other hand, substitutes the gaining of a credential or license at a single point in a career for a continuing process of independent review and mandated accomplishment replication.

The accountability process addresses this lack by insisting upon techniques and strategies which promote objectivity, feed back knowledge of results, and permit outside replication of demonstrated good practice. The recent inclusion of independent education accomplishment auditors in eighty-six school systems to verify locally derived objectives in Titles VII and VIII, the bilingual and dropout prevention programs of ESEA, is a practical manisfestation of this aspect of accountability.

Outside review tied to a public report probably explains the popularity of the emerging concept of accountability to the public at large. Schools in America serve and are accountable to the citizenry, not the professionals. Since the public served is in reality many "publics," each of whom has legitimate needs for information, accountability can lead to an opening up of the system to bring in new energy and new support.

Educational Engineering and Accountability

The process of change in education starts with the design or location of good practice and ends with the installation of that good practice in the classrooms and learning centers of the nation where it becomes standard practice. It is known that the change process involves adaptation of good practice and adoption. Educational engineering is the rapidly emerging field designed to produce personnel with competence in this change process. The development of this coherent body of knowledge and procedure represents a sixth powerful concomitant of accountability.

Since World War II, several fields have been developed to enable leaders of very complex enterprises to operate effectively and efficiently. These emerging fields include: system design and analysis, management by objectives, contract engineering (including warrantees, performance contracts, and incentives), logistics, quality assurance, value engineering, and the like. The coordination of these fields around educational concerns for an improved technology of instruction may be conveniently called education engineering.

Engineering has traditionally been a problem-solving activity, a profession dedicated to harnessing and creating technology to the accomplishment of desired ends, the resolution of difficulties, and the promotion of opportunities.

The heart of the education engineering process is the performance contract. Performance contracts are not new to education. But the concept of holding an educational agency accountable for results is. When a student is able to demonstrate in concrete terms what he has or has not learned, educators will be in a better position to judge where or why a program succeeds or fails and make the necessary changes to achieve success.

In the main, educators have not developed performance criteria for measuring the effectiveness of instructional programs, and many programs are now under way which do not describe what students are expected to gain from their educational experiences.

Instead of vague promises to provide students with an "appreciation of reading," instructional program objectives should be stated as is done in the national assessment program, in terms as specific as these in the following example:

> Given his state's written driving laws manual, a sample test and sufficient time, the student will be able to correctly answer 90 percent of the questions.

There are and should be larger objectives in education that are difficult to define and impossible to measure as the consequence of any given program. The "training" components of education, illustrated in the basic skills of reading, arithmetic, vocational training, and the like are amenable to performance contracts.

But the fact that many results of education are subjective and not measurable in the "hard," scientific sense should not deter personnel from dealing precisely with those aspects of education that lend themselves to precise definition and assessment. Rather, it demands that maximum use be made of those individual parts that tell what the change in the whole has been.

The Texarkana, Arkansas, performance contract of $80 for eighty hours of instruction with rewards for shorter time and penalties for non-achievement together with the Camp Mead use of a micro-society, learning center, and achievement motivation are striking examples.

Pursuit of accountability can be expected to cause substantive changes in the schools. A few of the probable changes are listed below. Since it is doubtful that results will be attained without some movement in the listed direction, commitment to accountability in education can be viewed as a commitment to better instructional practice. This is the final major powerful aspect of accountability that can be explored in this presentation.

Here are some of the expected changes in schools as a result of the call for accountability:

1. The teaching role will finally change from information-giving to directing learning. In many classrooms, the person who is active more than a fraction of the time is the teacher, who is generally doing the following:

   (a) Preparing and delivering lectures or talks to students whose motivation for paying attention or whose interest in what is being covered may be insufficient.

   (b) Preparing, administering, grading, and reviewing tests, assignments, and homework, and covering the textbook, which, because of the methods applied and the materials generally available have little value in helping the students to learn or the teachers to judge their own effectiveness.

2. The schools' facilities will become more open, more flexible, and less group-oriented. Students can learn as individuals or as members of a group. There are no alternatives in any specific learning situation. Group instruction has its values for motivation, for general direction, etc., but is contra-indicated for individual learning. The misuse of time and effort in attempting individual growth through sole or major reliance on group methods is monumental. Facilities encouraging individual instruction are essential in producing results.

3. The curriculum will become more relevant. When the emphasis moves from process to results, the whole environment becomes a source for schooling. "School" can then be held in businesses, homes, or through "bull" sessions. Teachers can be assisted by students and adults. Since the criterion is results, the process becomes open to a variety of input. Variety is the essence of motivation and can provide the realism so deeply desired by all who seek revelance in their schooling.

4. Outmoded myths and an incomplete educational tradition can be exposed and perhaps eliminated from the schools. Too much of the behavior toward children in school seems to reflect a "can't do" philosophy. Too many seem intent on proving that the bell-shaped curve, with its built-in reflection of failure, ought to be the symbol of education. Accountability for results will prime personnel toward a "can do" philosophy. They will be energized to try alternate ways if something isn't working. This change of attitude could be *the* major benefit of the concept of accountability.

Accountability in education may have substantive effects on two of the most pressing educational problems today: student unrest and boredom. Too often today the curriculum is a function of the materials and time. School personnel have the well-established use of textbooks as the chief teaching material and the idea that children have to go to school for approximately eight hours every weekday for roughly ten months a year. For too many, the chief characteristic of school can be listed as time serving, course taking, and credit getting.

Time serving is a basic cause of boredom. For, if time is standardized, one has to fill up. There is, unfortunately, a basic rhythm to time serving—the teacher introduces a topic, "teaches" it, gives an assignment, prepares for the test, gives the test, reviews the test, and then repeats the process until the course is *covered*—even if there is little mastery or great forgetting.

Many people with children in elementary schools, for example, have had their children out of school for extended periods of time for reasons of illness, moving, or vacations. It is not unusual for them to report that their children can miss half of the school year or even skip a year or more and still do the whole program without any difficulty. When time has to be filled, there is a tendency for incredible redundancy and repetition to appear. With over 20 percent mobility in the population, this insight is spreading to many of the patrons of the school system.

Results, criterion performances, striving toward valued and clearly communicated ends can change the climate and place time as a function of outcome. Accountability is not a panacea; it is a change in attitude and perspective. It is precisely the kind of change which many have been seeking.

Summary

The striking picture of the earth itself as a space vehicle, a counterpart of the space capsule from which the television cameras held in the hands of the astronaut beamed the pictures to television sets, gave an enormous segment of the population the lesson that those who live on the earth are stewards of the glorious home God has given. It is clear that we all are managers of precious and limited resources: a planet stocked with life and beauty and opportunity beyond telling; a heritage of freedom as Americans bought so dearly in the sacrifice and work and enterprise of those who went before. In the 1970's we all shall account for that stewardship.

It does not take prophetic vision to know that many of us will discover the very real connection between the lives we lead, the careers we pursue, the institutions we support, the thoughts we think, the values we hold, the priorities we attack, and our future as a people.

The first exercise in accountability must center on the care and nurture of our children. We are stewards of their education and training, and the education system we have created consists of more than the schools. Over the years we have gradually dispatched more and more of our personal responsibilities for the young to para-professional and professional strangers. The good and bad results of our stewardship are coming home for all to see and feel and experience.

Accountability runs counter to Larry Peter's principle. It jerks us up by the scruff of the neck to answer for our performance.

Perhaps the most fitting summary of the power and potential of accountability in American education can be gotten by considering its relationship to the unsettling change of which we are all so painfully aware.

We live in an age of massive, even shocking change. When men and women are bewildered by such change, our efforts *must* speak to then urgent problems. Developing and improving an educational system to enable people to cope with and to captain a society in the throes of intellectual, technological, and social revolutions far advanced is just such a problem.

Our time is marked, as Robert Oppenheimer once said in a Columbia University speech, by "the dissolution of authority in belief, in ritual, and in temporal order." It should not surprise us then that the school is not what it was, that there is great student unrest and patron dissatisfaction, and that the issue of relevance is a central issue in our professional life.

Professor Houston Smith, philosopher and teacher at M.I.T., has posed the issue of social change at its most poignant in his recent powerful and wise little book called *Condemned to Meaning*. Let me quote some of his insights.

> We live in a time when history appears to be rushing toward some sort of climax. New knowledge breaks over us with a force and constancy that sweeps us off our feet and keeps us from regaining them. Life's tempo quickens as if to the beat of a conductor crying, "Faster, faster." With moon travel we're prepared to make a pass at the infinite. With DNA we are thinking of retooling our offspring. What have we not done? What may we yet not do? . . . the future looks dazzling. Or rather, it would were it not for one thing: a growing question as to whether there's any point to the whole affair. For we are witness to one of the great ironies of history. The century which in the West has conquered disease, erased starvation, dispersed affluence, elongated life, and educated everybody, has generated in aggregate and average the gloomiest depiction of the human condition ever rendered. An occasional Greek wondered whether it might not have been better never to have been born, but an ingrowing pessimism seems to characterize most of our writers. Almost unvaryingly they depict a world that is meaningless or absurd. Open nearly any book, enter almost any theater, and "Life is a lie, my sweet. It builds green trees that ease your eyes and draw you under them. Then when you're here in the shade, and you breathe in and say, 'Oh God, how beautiful,' that's when the bird on the branch lets go his droppings and hits you on the head." Never have men known so much while doubting

whether it adds up to anything. Never has life been covertly so empty while overtly so full.

In the face of this void of meaning in our time, in this sustained crises of authority in our time, education must take on different dimensions. Accountability is the public policy declaration that speaks to those different dimensions. Engineering that policy into practical, vital programs is a matter of due urgency. Dr. Peter, bureaucrats, citizens, parents, board members, educators, and fellow Americans, take heed!

Accountability and the Teaching Profession

In our efforts to introduce the concept of accountability, we are aiming at improving the general educational process. Any examination of student performance should begin with an examination of the effectiveness of professional educators, especially the teachers and school administrators.

This chapter begins with a warning by Robert J. Havighurst that accountability directed solely at the teacher is oversimplified and dangerous. He contends that accountability must involve parents, teachers, school administrators, board members, taxpayers, and possibly students.

In the next section, David Selden warns that accountability models make teachers the scapegoats for the ills besetting education. Selden rejects the concept of accountability and maintains that its advocates approach education with ". . . all the insight of an irate viewer 'fixing' a television set: Give it a kick and see what happens."

W. James Popham then proposes a procedure for evaluating a teacher's effectiveness involving a teaching performance test. The instructional tasks being tested for would be held constant for all teachers, and all other relevant variables would also be controlled. Students would be assigned randomly to teachers, and, if necessary, any differences remaining in the learners' entry abilities and behaviors would be adjusted for statistically. This type of test, according to Popham, would provide an estimate of a teacher's ability to produce a given change in the performance of students.

In the final section, Hulda Grobman cautions that the clamor for accountability is forcing educators into a bind. Unreasonable demands for immediate
improvements have resulted in readily observable gains being stressed at the
expense of long-term, more important outcomes. Grobman takes issue with
the advocates of accountability who assume that schools know a great deal
about how children learn and that they know how to measure learning. She
feels that present knowledge in these two areas is limited, perhaps too
limited to permit the development of workable accountability models.

Joint Accountability:
A Constructive Response
to Consumer Demands

Robert J. Havighurst

In "the old days," a teacher's responsibility was limited to maintaining an orderly classroom in which pupils could concentrate on their schoolwork and "recite" what they had learned. It was understood that some pupils would fail, perhaps because they were "lazy" or "not bright," but that was their fault, or their nature, and they or their parents were responsible for their failure. The teacher was accountable for *teaching*, and the pupil was accountable for *learning*.

Now all that is changed. The teacher's hegemony in the classroom is challenged by three groups of people, each exerting a force on the school system:

1. Parents of unsuccessful pupils, who blame the teacher when their children do not make "normal" progress in school achievement. These parents have faith in education as a means of making their children successful in life, and they see that schooling is not living up to their expectations for their children.

2. Parents of children making good progress in school, who want them to do even better. They expect their children to compete more successfully for high marks on examinations in order to get into selective colleges and eventually to become more successful in life.

3. Taxpayers who feel the pinch of ever-rising tax bills for the support of public education. They want to know what they are getting for the additional outlay.

Even though these three groups are dissatisfied with teachers and the cost of schools, their complaints have not been taken seriously enough to cause major changes in the schools as long as there has been a shortage of teachers. Now, with the teacher shortage ended or ending, we are about to go into a period of emphasis by parents, school boards, and taxpayers on teacher accountability defined as *responsibility for what the student learns*. This is

Dr. Havighurst is Professor of Education and Human Development at The University of Chicago. This article originally appeared in *Nation's Schools* (May 1972). © Copyright 1972 by McGraw-Hill, Inc. Reprinted by permission.

a *pernicious* definition of teacher accountability, but the profession must cope with it during the next decade.

Why is it so pernicious? Because it places the whole weight of responsibility on only one of several agents who cause pupil success or failure. In addition to teacher efforts, these factors influence pupils' achievement:

1. The pupil's learning ability, which he brings with him to school.

2. The pupil's family—the experience and stimulation provided by the family in their conversation, reading habits, aspirations for the children, and models they provide for imitation by the child.

3. The pupil's peer group, which sets standards of acceptable performance in various areas of behavior and teaches values and aspirations.

4. The local community, which provides models through its leading citizens and reflects expectation of a certain level of knowledge and of intellectual activity.

5. The school board, which is legally responsible for the facilities and policies of the school system.

6. The pupil's self-concept, aspirations, ambitions, and interests.

In view of the complexity of these causal agents, any simple system of accountability is likely to be a bad one. The simple systems fall into the trap of defining accountability as personal responsibility of the teacher, or the principal, or the pupil. The following example of a "bad" system does not actually exist anywhere, but it illustrates the dangers inherent in the oversimplified concept of accountability as a personal responsibility of the teacher.

This plan ties teacher pay to pupil achievement. It assumes that the teacher's effort and skill are the main elements producing school achievement and that adoption of the plan will produce immediate improvement in achievement.

Under the plan, all teachers would be paid 90 percent of their basic salary monthly. For example, a teacher with a salary of $8,000, ordinarily paid in ten monthly installments, would receive $720 rather than $800 per month. At the end of the school year, he would receive additional payment based on pupil achievement. Payment would be computed as follows:

1. Measure the achievement level of the teacher's class at the beginning of the school year with standardized tests in reading and arithmetic.

2. Measure the achievement level of the class at the end of the year with similar tests.

3. Compute the average gain of the class in tenths of a year, *e.g.* the class average increases from 5.2 to 6.0 during the year, reflecting a .8 gain.

4. Pay the teacher a sum determined by multiplying one-tenth of the year's salary ($800) by the number of tenths of a year his class gained. A teacher whose class gained .8 of a year on the standardized tests, for example, would

be paid .8 of $800 or $640; a teacher whose class gained 1.4 years would be paid $1,120. Thus a teacher whose class gained more than a year (the national average) on standardized tests would receive a final payment totaling more than the amount of his withheld salary, and a teacher whose class gained less than a year would get less than his original salary.

Foremost among objections to such a plan is that it would penalize a teacher with a class of disadvantaged students, who seldom make a year's progress on a standard test. Equally unfair, it would reward a teacher with a class of well-to-do pupils, who usually gain more than a year. Mainly for this reason, any accountability scheme which ties teacher pay to the performance level of pupils is likely to be opposed by teachers.

If my analysis of the situation is fairly accurate, the public will put so much pressure on the teaching profession for an accounting that one of two things will happen:

1. The teaching profession will try to blunt the pressure by reducing its claims on the public purse and saying that expenditures on schooling beyond certain limits produce diminishing returns. It will state that family and community factors contribute so much to the child's educational achievement that the school's contribution has just about reached its practicable limit for middle-class children.

Although some hard-headed critics of contemporary formal education can amass considerable evidence to support this view of the limited effectiveness of schooling, most educators would disagree vehemently. They would argue that better education can be provided, that more schooling is good for society, and that the current but dwindling oversupply of teachers will quickly be absorbed by reducing the pupil-teacher ratio to 24 to 1, thus improving the quality of the schools.

2. A system of *joint accountability* among the several social systems and groups of people who have a legitimate interest and responsibility for the education of children and youth will be worked out. Joint accountability would involve active participation from teachers, administrators, the school board, parents, citizens and taxpayers, and possibly the students.

How are teachers to hold themselves accountable under a system of joint accountability? Perhaps their professional organizations might adopt the following procedure for evaluating a teacher and a school faculty. Data would be collected and teachers evaluated concerning:

1. Knowledge of the local community obtained through formal or informal study of the community, through home visits, etc.

2. Knowledge of the pupils in the teacher's classroom, based on observation of the pupils and study of their records.

3. A plan for the year's program, based on knowledge of the community and the pupils.

4. Control of pupils' classroom behavior—is the classroom a place that encourages effective schoolwork by pupils?

5. General use of school facilities—library, art room, laboratories, etc.

6. Efforts to relate pupils to the local community for educational purposes.

7. A survey of pupil behavior—in the classroom, in the halls, on the playground. Is it purposeful, productive, reasonably orderly?

8. Test data on school achievement, taken at the beginning and end of the school year.

A confidential report evaluating each teacher on these items would be issued to the teacher annually. The teacher's salary would be independent of the evaluation process, although the evaluation would influence the teacher's behavior and would have a major bearing on his career.

To work democratically, a system of joint accountability would require candid and careful self-evaluation by members of the other social systems involved with the school. The parents' organization would have to work out procedures for examining itself and for reporting on itself to the community. For example, a local school advisory council elected by parents would have to accept responsibility for looking critically at teachers. Similarly, a citywide citizens school committee or taxpayers association would assume its share of responsibility for the maintenance and improvement of the educational system and would solicit a critical evaluation of the performance of its functions.

For a good system of accountability to be developed, it must be spearheaded by local administrators and teachers. They must take the lead in defining their own accountability and, at the same time, helping parents and citizens to understand their input into the educational process, to evaluate their performance, and to learn what they can reasonably expect from the schools. Nothing less is acceptable.

Productivity, Yes.
Accountability, No.

David Selden

It's no mystery why teachers regard the present public outcry for "account-ability" as an unwarranted slur on their motives and abilities.

For one thing, most teachers are trying desperately to fulfill their assigned tasks. The small proportion of goof-offs in education affects productivity much less than gross defects of the system stemming from years of financial malnutrition.

For another, "accountability" seems to have as many definitions as there are definers. The rationale advanced by Leon Lessinger, originator of the term as applied to education, is that education is becoming more and more expensive, and yet there is no way to show that we are getting more for our money. As a matter of fact, he says, the available evidence shows that we are actually getting less. Before more money is put into schools, equipment and personnel, he adds, a way must be found to make sure we're getting our money's worth.

But when we think "schools," we almost automatically think "teachers." Thus accountability offers ready teacher scapegoats to amateur and professional school haters, from the fellow who did not get along well with his eighth-grade teacher to the corporation executive who judges schools by his company's property tax rate. It is this accusatory aspect of accountability that sets teachers' teeth on edge.

Significantly, most accountability advocates want to do away with the due process protections of teacher tenure acts established after years of hard work in the state legislatures. If a child is not learning, it must be the teacher's fault, these advocates say, so teachers should "shape up or ship out." Never mind what kind of out-of-school problems the child has or any of the other possible physical or emotional impediments to learning.

An example of this "get the teacher" attitude of the accountability pro-motors is the famous "Clark Plan" drawn up for Washington, D. C., schools two years ago by Kenneth Clark, well-known social psychologist. Clark recommended that a series of standardized tests be given to all District children at regular intervals. If students did not make equivalent academic advancement, their teachers would be "counseled with." Teacher pay would be based on student achievement.

Mr. Selden is president of the American Federation of Teachers, AFL-CIO. This article originally appeared in *Nation's Schools* (May 1972). © Copyright 1972 by McGraw-Hill, Inc. Reprinted by permission.

The concept of accountability, of course, is not limited to education these days, and the idea is not all bad. Consumer advocates such as Ralph Nader and his student associates have been trying to force vast corporations which have long operated on a "let-the-buyer-beware" basis to become publicly responsible. But accountability in the auto industry is much different from accountability in education. If a car's brakes fail, management gets the blame. It is assumed that the design was faulty, or that the company cut too many corners in reducing costs. But if a child does not learn to read, the assumption is that his teacher, rather than the managers of the educational system, did not do a good job.

There is a great deal of "know-nothingism" in the approach of the account-abilitarians. They do not tell us how accountability will change current teaching methods. They do not even advocate any particular philosophic underpinning for their theory, nor can they diagram a reorganization of school structure or curriculum. They approach education with all the insight of an irate viewer "fixing" a telivision set: Give it a kick and see what happens. No consideration is given to the possibility that education—teaching and learning—may be a complex and largely unexplored region requiring the cooperative effort of everyone involved if success is to be achieved.

The most egregious development of the accountability movement is performance contracting, a concept that outrages most teachers.

In the first place, teachers believe they have never been given a chance to succeed with traditional methods. "How can we really teach thirty disadvantaged kids at a time in these days of crime, drug addiction, and social unrest," they ask, "especially when we have to handle thirty classroom hours a week?" Their reasoning is borne out by experiences in the various high-staff-ratio elementary programs such as New York City's More Effective Schools, Chicago's READ program, and the Neighborhood Educational Centers in Detroit.

In these schools the staffing ratio permits class size limits of no more than twenty children per teacher, and teachers have a couple of free periods every day to use for consultation with colleagues, work with individual children, lesson planning, marshalling instructional materials, and just plain rest. And the children learn—not just memorized "answers" but a whole range of ego-strengthening attitudes and convictions.

The rhetoric of performance contracting adherents, however, makes no allowances for such rational considerations. "Education has failed," they say. "Spending more money for richer staffing ratios is merely adding 'more of the same.' Let's try something new." The "percon" peddlers also promise to produce more education for the same amount of money now being spent. "Don't pay us if the pupils don't learn," they say. It is the old money-back guarantee applied to schooling. Boards of education and parents can hardly be blamed for taking a flyer on it. After all, children are not learning as things are now.

The facts show, however, that performance contracting not only costs more money but also produces insignificant student achievement gains. Not to mention the management problems it invites by employing footloose staffing procedures.

Are there other ways, perhaps less objectionable than performance contracting, to build accountability into education? One suggestion is to encourage much closer surveillance of schools by local communities. But, again, the educational results are apt to be pretty bad. A conflict between aroused community groups and teachers, for example, was responsible for the 37-day teacher strike in New York City in the fall of 1968.

Another form of teacher accountability is closer supervision. Like any other workers, teachers resent the breathing-over-your-shoulder type of "snoopervision" which some overzealous administrators employ. When supervision is used merely to put pressure on already overburdened teachers, the result will be a teacher rebellion if the practice is widespread.

Is there *any* sort of accountability that teachers would approve of? In the United Federation of Teachers (New York City) contract, ratified in June, 1969, the school board and the union agreed to develop such a plan, and a fund was set aside to employ competent resource people. The job was turned over to Educational Testing Service of Princeton, N.J. After more than two years of study, ETS has to come up with a viable plan—not because it could not get the cooperation of teachers; rather, it could not develop a plan in which the testing service itself could have confidence.

We are just beginning to get to the bottom of some of the problems involved in the learning process. Conceivably it may be possible at some time in the future to computerize individual teacher productivity so that the public will know what a teacher is putting out, but when we reach that stage, few teachers will want to stay in the profession. Good teaching is a creative acitivity as well as a production process.

Much of the rhetoric of accountability seems to stem directly from "the cult of efficiency in education." We have always treated education as a mass production industry. One of the basic principles of mass production is to so simplify the task of each worker that his function can be learned in a very short time without any previous training. Our educational factories are designed to be operated by nice young ladies working under the supervision of somewhat sterner older ladies and gentlemen.

Although no school should refuse to adopt new methods that will make a teacher's work more productive, it must be careful not to use the term "productivity" as loosely as "accountability" is used. The American educational enterprise has been marvelously productive on a unit-cost basis, but at the expense of children who have been shunted aside because they do not conform to the educational assembly line. If the system expects to increase productivity in terms of "gross national education product," it will have to come up with more capital investment and manpower.

Instead of looking for ways to build in incentives and other efficiency devices, we would be better advised to discover ways to humanize the system. The British have pioneered in this direction. The British infant schools are the very antithesis of what accountabilitarians would have us do. Yet these schools produce good education with little strain.

Another British device that could improve teacher productivity is the "teacher center." Most people who have studied education have come to the conclusion that nothing good happens in schools unless teachers make it happen. Productivity cannot be improved by piling on more oppressive supervision. Rather, teachers must be given the responsibility for working out their own best methods of teaching. In the teacher center, teachers meet and confer with each other, learn about new techniques, and watch demonstrations.

And now we come to the real nub of the accountability question. Teachers do not mind being held accountable for things over which they have some control. For instance, all teachers accept the idea that they must come to school on time, must plan lessons, must be as responsive as possible to student needs. But teachers bitterly resent having to teach in overcrowded classrooms, handle the emotional problems of disturbed children, and work without proper supplies and instructional materials. These are all matters that fall within the province of administrators, school boards, and the taxpayers. Teachers gain a semblance of control over such conditions only by exerting great collective effort.

Accountability is a two-way street. If teachers are to be accountable to the public, the public must be accountable to teachers. James Coleman identified most of the major influences on pupil achievement, and by far the most potent were environmental factors. Our teachers must be given the resources to overcome the crippling effects on children of the defects in our society—unemployment, racism, drug addiction, alcoholism, and the brutality of poverty. If we are really interested in increasing productivity rather than mere finger-pointing and scapegoating, let us develop ways in which teachers can share policymaking responsibilities. We have much more to gain by enhancing the opportunities for cooperation than by introducing the two-edged sword of accountability.

Found: A Practical Procedure to Appraise Teacher Achievement in the Classroom

W. James Popham

Talk is cheap. While everyone's talking about the merits of educational accountability, few mention the fact that practical procedures for making accountability work have not been devised.

Tangible suggestions for implementing accountability systems have been made, however. One of the most interesting concerns is the use of the teaching performance test, a specific measurement tactic that can be employed in various accountability approaches.

Since the turn of the century, how to measure a teacher's instructional skill has perplexed a stream of educational researchers and evaluators. The most widely used measures—ratings, classroom observations, and pupil performance on standardized tests—all have proved dismally inadequate. They too often have been process-focused. They have tried to isolate "good teaching techniques" even though subsequent research strongly suggests that few, if any, pedagogical ploys invariably will work in all the instructional settings teachers encounter. If not process-focused, these measurement techniques often have failed to take into account the fact that different teachers pursue markedly different goals.

To eliminate some of these difficulties, a previously untried assessment technique, the teaching performance test, has been tested experimentally since 1965. While considerable research remains to be conducted on various aspects of teaching performance tests, results of their use in field trials suggest that they warrant further utilization.

A teaching performance test provides a prespecified behavior change in a group of appropriate learners. Here's how it functions:

1. A teacher is given an explicit instructional objective along with a sample measurement item showing how the objective's achievement will be measured. He also receives background information on the objective.

2. The teacher gets time to read the background information (if necessary) and to plan a lesson designed to achieve the objective.

Dr. Popham is Professor of Education at UCLA. This article originally appeared in *Nation's Schools* (May 1972). © Copyright 1972 by McGraw-Hill, Inc. Reprinted by permission.

3. The teacher instructs a group of pupils—as few as a half dozen or as many as a whole class—for a specified period of time.

4. The pupils are measured with a post-test based on the objective but unseen previously by the teacher. Pupil attitudes toward the instruction also are measured. These measures of pupil cognitive and affective results serve as an index of the teacher's effectiveness.

In general, the subject matter employed for each performance test is novel, thereby reducing the likelihood of the learner's previous familiarity with the topic. Because the same instructional objective is employed for all teachers completing a given performance test, legitimate comparisons can be made among different teachers' skill in accomplishing the preset objectives. This, of course, is the new measurement angle. By holding the instructional task constant, it is possible to contrast the ability of different teachers to get their pupils to master the task and demonstrate positive affect toward the instruction.

The trick, clearly, is to control other relevant conditions so that all teachers have the same opportunity to display whatever instructional skill they possess. This means randomly assigning learners to teachers and, if necessary, statistically adjusting for remaining inequities in disparate learners' entry behavior.

Right now teaching performance tests can play two valuable and practical roles in educational accountability systems. They can be used for *instructional improvement*—to help teachers get better at promoting beneficial changes in learners. And they can be employed for *skill assessment*—to discover which teachers are particularly good or particularly bad at this type of instructional task.

In the case of *personal* educational accountability, in which the teacher initiates any review of the results of his instruction, a teacher might use a performance test chiefly for instructional improvement. Either by himself or with invited colleagues, a teacher might work with different groups of children for short periods after school in successive efforts to improve his skill on a particular performance test or on a certain class of performance tests. Lessons that failed to achieve the objective or that promoted negative learner affect would be revised.

For *professional* accountability systems, in which a group of the teacher's colleagues initiates a review of his instruction, teaching performance tests can be employed for both instructional improvement and skill assessment. Groups of teachers, for example, might wish to foster the use of performance tests to help their colleagues get better at accomplishing instructional objectives. Teachers might be required by their colleagues to participate in a series of performance test clinics that featured post-lesson clinical analyses of the teachers' instructional decisions.

More important, perhaps, is the possibility that teacher organizations will seize upon the use of teaching performance tests as a skill assessment device to accomplish what they have always sought—control over entry into the profession. Consistent with a general thrust for professional responsibility, teacher organizations might set up procedures obliging aspiring teachers to display, along with other abilities, at least a minimum level of skill on teaching performance tests.

Finally, for *public* accountability systems, in which evidence regarding the quality of learner attainments is demanded by the public, the skill assessment use of performance tests may have merit. In an effort to make school systems answer for results, it is certainly plausible that the public might demand that teachers display at least minimal proficiency on performance tests.

The skill assessment approach also might help administrators select the most competent teachers applying for jobs. Administrators could set up a series of teaching performance tests, requiring three or four hours' time, to be completed by all applicants. This type of screening examination would be similar to the procedure whereby applicants for a given graduate school must complete, at their personal expense, the Graduate Record Examination. And since enrichment topics could be used for the performance test subject matter, any pupils from the district who participated in this screening process would be gaining new and useful knowledge.

As these illustrations have shown, the reason that the teaching performance test strategy should be particularly useful to proponents of educational accountability systems is its complete congruence with the central assumption of all accountability systems—a focus on the outcomes of instruction. To be sure, teaching performance tests assess only one competency of a teacher—his ability to achieve prespecified objectives. While that is only one criterion that should be used in evaluating a teacher, *it is a critical criterion.* Insofar as one believes the mission of teachers is to change children for the better, then any indicator of a teacher's skill in doing so should be given careful consideration.

Some will say, "But this isn't what teaching is really like. Teaching for a full day with thirty-five kids in a classroom is vastly different from teaching eight randomly assigned learners for a thirty-minute lesson." Of course there are differences. But is there any reason to believe that a teacher who has performed miserably on several short-term performance tests will suddenly blossom in a regular teaching situation? Hardly.

Accountability for What?

Hulda Grobman

To reject the idea of accountability is tantamount to saying that the schools and their personnel are not and should not be responsible for what they do, thus implying that schools and their personnel are responsible to no one. This is an untenable position both in terms of the educators' moral responsibility and, more practically, from the standpoint of the public's control of its schools. The principle of accountability is unquestionable. But open to serious debate is the question: Accountability for what? What are—or should be—the areas of accountability and the criteria used to measure achievement?

Schools are multipurpose institutions. They have clusters of aims that they expect to achieve within specific spans of time—that is, they are concerned with multiple outcomes anticipated at different times, such as at the end of a unit, semester, year, level of schooling; at the end of all schooling; or in later adult years. They also have a variety of focuses for their goals. Thus, even though they may differ widely in subject-area coverage, all schools have some knowledge-oriented goals that cover reading, writing, arithmetic, and other subject-matter areas. Schools must also deal with demands for the development of such intellectual skills as problem solving, inquiry-oriented exploration, learning how to learn, critical thinking, and evaluating data, arguments and positions.

Interpersonal skills, including socialization, communication, and cooperation, are commonly agreed upon as desirable goals, though the precise parameters of these skills may vary from one school to another. There are also value-oriented or affective outcomes that the school is responsible for, including motivation for learning, sense of responsibility, commitment to a democratic ideal, adequate self-image, positive attitude toward school and learning, and commitment to rationality in solving personal and public problems. The development of psychomotor skills is implicitly or explicitly expected, and these skills involve gross and fine muscle coordination in manipulative skills. Such intellectual skills as reading and writing, for example, require fine muscular or psychomotor skills, though these are frequently not specifically identified in outlining goals.

Dr. Grobman is Professor of Education at New York University. Most of this article originally appeared in *Nation's Schools* (May 1972). ©Copyright 1972 by McGraw-Hill, Inc. Reprinted by permission.

Although the way in which individual schools or school systems interpret their goals varies, it is nonetheless possible for schools to translate them into specific behavioral or nonbehavioral objectives, for long-term, intermediate, and immediate attainment—that is, for general end-of-schooling attainment, year-long attainment, or day, week, or unit attainment.

By their very nature, short-term and intermediate goals are simply vehicles for achieving long-term goals. For example, attaining on-grade-level reading achievement for a class at Grade 2 is not an end in itself, but this achievement represents an important way station in an eventual higher degree of literacy. In the context of a given school and grade level, the focus of accountability must be on readily measurable short-term and intermediate aims—that is, on the achievement of goals that may be measured during the school year. Such measurement assumes that end-of-year measurement of a relatively short-term aim represents measurement of progress in achieving the long-run aim. Further, it assumes that the achievement of measurable or measured aims is accompanied by a parallel achievement of non-measurable aims. These assumptions should be carefully considered, because if any is invalid, the validity of any accountability system is jeopardized.

At the present time we do not know how to measure the attainment of many of the things we are concerned with in education. We have no compelling evidence to indicate that sufficient correlation exists between those goals that can be measured and those that cannot be measured to enable the former to serve as an adequate indicator of the latter. Further, educators rarely make systematic analyses of the assumptions underlying the implication of such a connection, nor do they examine the logic of such assumptions.

Thus, many educators assume that mastering a vocabulary or a series of concepts is the natural and logical precurser of the ability to reason out future problems. Demonstrating the ability to use a microscope, to list five causes of World War I, or to parse a sentence is tacitly assumed to enhance the individual's later scientific literacy, his ability to cope with public issues of the future, or his use of grammatical English. Unfortunately, not only is there little evidence to substantiate these assumptions, but we have substantial evidence that makes any prediction of such outcomes questionable. For example, several studies have found no positive correlation between scores on traditional tests that are knowledge-oriented and those on tests that simulate real-life situations and require the retrieval of this information, sorting it out, and applying it in a new, complex situation.[1] Yet most school tests, including those used for accountability purposes, reflect only a knowledge-oriented focus.

---

[1]Christine McGuire and David Babbott, "Simulation Technique in the Measurement of Problem Solving Situations," *Journal of Educational Measurement* (Spring 1967): pp. 1–10.

The activities involved in producing short-term learnings are often accompanied by by-product learnings that may interfere with later learning or with the use of what has been learned. For example, in junior and senior high school, students often exhibit serious anxiety about math and they often dislike math more than most other subjects. It seems clear that this situation reflects their earlier experiences with math. They show a notable lack of initiative in applying their previously acquired math skills to new situations. In adult years, the inability of many supermarket shoppers to figure out unit costs of groceries—a computational task taught in the elementary grades—is obvious. In this connotation, have the early experiences in math—even if they produced desired short-term math skills—been effective ones? And, to add a different dimension, when a high school attempts to measure the adequacy of its math teaching, should it be penalized for the attitudes that the students developed in earlier grades?

Even the tests we use to gauge progress may, in fact, be counterproductive when considered in terms of some larger objectives of education. A reading test with dull pedestrian passages does not contribute to the aim of learning that reading is important and can be a source of joy and excitement. A test of facts related to science does not contribute to the notion that science is interesting and provides a way of finding out new things. Probably, obverse results are being achieved. In such instances students learn from the test situations that school is dull and irrelevant; that teachers say one thing (problem solving and inquiry are important) but test another (memory)—which is to say teachers cannot be trusted; that learning is not a pleasant activity, but an anxiety-producing one that may even be used as punishment ("You can't go out to play until you finish learning your . . .").

If teachers are threatened with accountability measures that focus on short-term measurable goals, their only recourse is to stress in class what is stressed in the accountability measures, frequently to the detriment of more important learnings. And this focus may carry highly inappropriate concomitant learnings. Thus, the widely publicized instances of teaching for specific tests in several schools with performance contracting is probably an unfortunate harbinger of things to come.

Further, the focus on some subject areas and skills to be tested may lead educators to underemphasize or overlook other areas of outcomes that are not being measured. Such skills as socialization, cooperation, and communication (if they are not measured—and they are not usually measured in accountability systems) will undoubtedly suffer. What is measured becomes important in the minds of the teachers and the students. If memory is measured but inquiry-oriented exploration is not, or if rote learning is measured but such abilities as learning how to learn and building healthy self-concepts are not, it is clear where the teaching emphasis will be. By utilizing such criteria for accountability, the school is indicating more clearly in deed than it ever could in words what its priorities are. And teachers and students will certainly be affected by them.

Accountability will undoubtedly influence teacher-student relationships. When teachers are under stress to show a given level of results, what will be the consequences for the student who, through no fault of his own, does not meet the expected standard? How will the school and the teachers feel about him? And how much of this feeling will come through to him?

It would be interesting to speculate on how schools might be different if, rather than focusing on the results of achievement tests, the criteria of success included data on frequency of stomach ulcers, psychological problems, and unduly high anxiety levels in students, as well as measures of self-reliance, sense of responsibility, creativity and non-authoritarian attitudes. And whether, in fact, student progress based on such criteria as these would contribute more to the achievement of the schools' long-term aims than does progress on achievement tests.

Inherent in the principle of accountability is the need for valid prediction of performance; that is, before we can determine if outcomes are up to standard, it is necessary to predict a reasonable level of expectation for a given school, class, or the individuals within a class. This is extremely difficult.

For example, it might appear that a reasonable expectation in reading gain for a class at any grade level from 1 through 12, in any school might be a minimum of at least one year in the course of a school year. However, such an expectation would reflect an overly simplistic view of human development and learning. It ignores some of the important things we know about individuals and how they develop and how they learn. For example, all learning is based on prior learning and on prior and present environments in and out of school. Bloom cites an estimate that 33 percent of development of general learning takes place from birth to age 6, before the child enters first grade; 17 percent takes place from ages 9 through 12. From this he concludes: "We are inclined to believe that this [up to age 9] is the most important growing period for academic achievement and that *all subsequent learning in the school is affected and in large part determined by what the child has learned by the age of 9 or by the end of grade 3.*"[2]

This does not mean that once a learning deficit occurs remediation is impossible. But it does clearly imply that some learning deficits are far more difficult to overcome than others. Thus, deficits in reading or arithmetic or other subject-matter skills provide far different remediation problems in early

[2]Benjamin S. Bloom, *Stability and Change in Human Characteristics* (New York: John Wiley & Sons, 1964), p. 110. (Italics added).

elementary grades than in middle school or junior high school, and these same deficits would provide problems of still different dimensions at the senior high school level. Further, a sixth grade class with a one-year average deficit in reading and a range of reading scores from 4 to 8 provides a different and probably less difficult change deficit problem than the sixth grade class with the same average deficit in reading but with a range from grades 2 to 8. Our information on the extent to which intellectual deficits of one maturation period can be made up in another is very limited and we cannot now precisely equate differences in difficulty in reversing deficits of different magnitudes or at different stages of intellectual development.

Reasonable prediction is further complicated by the fact that the child and his learning patterns are inextricably related to his total school and non-school environment. A great many out-of-school variables are known to directly affect learning—family stability, economic and educational levels, nutrition, and the child's environment to the extent it provides him with stimulating experiences. Although many variables are beyond the school's control, they directly influence the child's learning rate, and it is unrealistic to predict learning outcomes without considering them.

Thus, comparable teaching inputs result in differential outputs depending on current and pre-existing environmental variables beyond the control of the individual teacher and school. The accurate prediction of these outputs is not possible at our present stage of knowledge. We simply cannot now set reliable, specific benchmarks in terms of relative difficulty in achieving gains for different individuals or groups of individuals in different environments. We only know that such differences exist and that they constitute highly significant variables in learning. Recognition of the need for differential benchmarks does not mean that all children should not learn to read adequately; it *does* mean that a given input of teaching enables them to do so far more readily at one level or in one situation than in another.

Accountability involves problems of defining goals, interaction among different kinds of goals and priorities among goals, limitations on measurements of many important goals, and the complexity of variables affecting learning. An easy reaction to these problems and limitations is to say that all these things can be worked out. Perhaps they can when we have learned more about measurement and about the differential effects of various environmental factors on learning. But the fact is that, to date, these problems have *not* been worked out. The result is that teachers and school administrators are being placed in a performance bind, where unreasonable demands are being made, where school patrons hold unreasonable expectations, and where, as a result, short-term readily observable gains are being sought at the cost of long-term, more important outcomes.

Does this mean that accountability cannot be considered until more realistic measures of all outcomes of education are available? No. A great deal can be learned through tentative realistic steps toward accountability. But this can best be done when there is a recognition of the limitations of our measures; an appreciation that learning to read, to count, to spell is a complex thing; and an awareness that learning involves more than the *goodness* of the teacher or even of the school system.

Accountability implies that the school knows a great deal about individuals and how and when they learn most readily; therefore, it can provide reasonable expectations in terms of each individual for each kind of performance that should be assessed. Unless all this can be done, the motto of the school implementing accountability might well be, "I'd rather have my facts all wrong than have no facts whatever."[3]

Accountability is undoubtedly necessary and desirable. But given our present limitations of knowledge about learning, about ways of measuring all-important outcomes, and about the complex relationship between short-term and long-term outcomes, the implementation of accountability procedures today would probably do far more harm than good to the children in our schools.

[3]Ogden Nash, "Who Did Which Or, Who Indeed?" *Bed Riddance* (New York: Little, Brown, and Co., 1969), p. 22.

Accountability Proposals and Methods

If accountability is to be a useful tool in education, realistic and workable procedures to implement it must be devised. The plans must clearly define who will be held accountable and how the major variables affecting teaching and learning, including those that operate outside the schools, will be measured. This is no easy task and few educators have developed comprehensive plans that deal with all of these problems. To date, the two most sophisticated accountability plans have been proposed by Henry S. Dyer and Stephen M. Barro. The complexity of their plans will be apparent to most readers, but the ideas expressed are important and worth a careful perusal.

Dyer's plan includes four major variables: (1) input (characteristics of students), (2) the educational process (activities in school organized to bring about desirable changes), (3) surrounding conditions (home, community, and school), and (4) output (characteristics of students as they emerge from a particular phase of their schooling). These four variables and their respective components are interrelated and, when measured, produce indices by which the effectiveness of the educational process can be judged.

The plan proposed by Barro includes a method for separating the impact of the teacher's actions on student performance from the effects of non-teaching variables as part of the procedures for determining the extent to which the performance of students is attributable to the actions of the teachers. This same kind of plan can be used to determine the effectiveness of different schools, and by adjusting for these differences, to assess the performance of the school's administrators. The problems posed by omitted variables, possible correlations between supposedly independent variables, and models that are too simple to take account of some of the important relationships among school inputs and outputs are also examined.

Felix M. Lopez discusses some misconceptions underlying many accountability programs and the reasons for their failure, and suggests some prerequisites for success. He believes that accountability should be based on a charter, containing a statement of the specific purposes, goals, and objectives of the school system, its various divisions and personnel.

Toward Objective Criteria of Professional Accountability in the Schools

Henry S. Dyer

The Concept of Professional Accountability

The concept of accountability can have many levels of meaning, depending upon where one focuses attention in the structure of the school system. Throughout this paper I shall be using the term in a restricted sense as it applies to the individual school as a unit. At this level I think of the concept as embracing three general principles:

1. The professional staff of a school is to be held collectively responsible for *knowing* as much as it can (a) about the intellectual and personal-social development of the pupils in its charge and (b) about the conditions and educational services that may be facilitating or impeding the pupils' development.

2. The professional staff of a school is to be held collectively responsible for *using* this knowledge as best it can to maximize the development of its pupils toward certain clearly defined and agreed-upon pupil performance objectives.

3. The board of education has a corresponding responsibility to provide the means and technical assistance whereby the staff of each school can acquire, interpret, and use the information necessary for carrying out the two foregoing functions.

I emphasize the notion of *joint accountability* of the entire school staff in the aggregate—principal, teachers, specialists—because it seems obvious that what happens to any child in a school is determined by the multitude of transactions he has with many different people on the staff who perform differing roles and presumably have differing impacts on his learning, which cannot readily, if ever, be disentangled. I emphasize the notion that staff members are to be held accountable for keeping themselves informed about the diverse needs of their pupils and for doing the best they can to meet those needs. In light of what we still don't know about the teaching-learning process, this

Dr. Dyer is Senior Advisor to Educational Testing Service, Princeton, N.J. This article originally appeared in *Phi Delta Kappan* (December 1970). Copyright ©1970 by Phi Delta Kappa, Inc. Reprinted by permission.

is the most one may reasonably expect. To hold teachers, or anybody else, accountable for delivering some sort of "guaranteed pupil performance" is likely to do more harm than good in the lives of the children. Finally, I emphasize that professional accountability should be seen as a two-way street, wherein a school staff is to be held accountable to higher authority for its own operations while the higher authorities in turn are to be held accountable for supplying the appropriate information and facilities each school staff requires to operate effectively.

An important implication in the three principles set forth above is that there shall be developed a district-wide educational accounting system optimally adaptable to the information needs of each school in the district. Later on I shall describe the salient features of such a system and shall suggest the procedures by which it might be developed and put to use. In this connection it should be noted that the type of *educational* accounting system here contemplated is to be distinguished from a *fiscal* accounting system. The kind of information provided by the former should not be confused with the kind provided by the latter. At all levels, the two types should complement each other in an overall management information system capable of relating benefits to costs. At the individual school level, however, educational accounting per se is of prime importance and is not usefully related to fiscal accounting, since the staff in a single school does not have and, in ordinary circumstances, cannot have much if any latitude in the raising and expending of funds for its local operations.

The next section outlines what a fully functioning educational accounting system might be like and how it could operate as a means for holding a school staff accountable, within certain constraints, for continually improving the effectiveness of its work. The last section briefly sketches plans by which the system might be brought into being and contains some cautions that should be heeded along the way.

Characteristics of an Educational Accounting System

The theory behind the first of the three principles stated in the preceding section is that if a school staff is to fulfill its professional obligations it must have extensive knowledge of the pupils it is expected to serve. This theory is based on the notion of a school as a social system that effects changes of various kinds in both the children who pass through it and in the professional personnel responsible for maintaining the school. The school as a social system becomes an educational system when its constituents are trying to ensure that all such changes shall be for the better. That is, the school as a *social* system becomes an *educational* system when its constituents—pupils, teachers, principal—are working toward some clearly defined pupil performance objectives.

There are four groups of variables in the school as a social system that must be recognized and measured if one is to develop acceptable criteria of staff accountability. These four groups of variables I call *input, educational process, surrounding conditions,* and *output.* Taken together, they form the pupil-change model of a school.

The *input* to any school at any given level consists of the characteristics of the pupils as they enter that level of their schooling: their health and physical condition, their skill in the three R's, their feelings about themselves and others, their aspirations, and so on. (Note the restriction of meaning of the term *input* as used here. It does *not* include such variables as per-pupil expenditure, institutional effort, facilities, and the like.) The *output* of any school consists of the same characteristics of the pupils as they emerge from that particular phase of their schooling some years later.

According to this conception, the input to any school consists of the output from the next lower level. Thus, the output of an elementary school becomes the input for junior high, and the output of junior high becomes the input for senior high. It is important to note that the staff of an individual school which is not in a position to select the pupils who come to it has no control over the level or quality of its input. In such a case, the pupil input represents a *fixed condition* with which the school staff must cope. The pupil output, however, is a variable that depends to some extent on the quality of service the school provides.

The third group of variables in the pupil-change model consists of the *surrounding conditions* within which the school operates. These are the factors in the school environment that may influence, for better or for worse, how teachers teach and pupils learn. The surrounding conditions fall into three categories: home conditions, community conditions, and school conditions. Home conditions include such matters as the level of education of the pupils' parents, the level of family income, the family pressures, and the physical condition of the home. Community conditions include the density of population in the enrollment area, the ethnic character of the population, the number and quality of available social agencies, the degree of industrialization, and so on. School conditions include the quality of the school plant, pupil-teacher ratio, classroom and playground footage per pupil, the *esprit de corps* of the staff, and the like.

In respect to all three types of surrounding conditions, one can distinguish those that the staff of a school finds easy to change from those that it finds hard to change. For example, in respect to home conditions, the school staff is hardly in a position to change the socioeconomic level of pupils' parents, but it may well be in a position to change the parents' attitudes toward education through programs that involve them in the work of the school. Similarly, in respect to school conditions, it might not be able to effect much change in the classroom footage per pupil, but it could probably develop programs that might influence the *esprit de corps* of the staff through in-service training. The identification of hard-to-change as contrasted with easy-to-change surrounding conditions is of the utmost importance in working toward objective criteria of professional accountability, since the staff of a school can hardly be held accountable for changing those factors in its situation over which it has little or no control.

The final set of variables in the pupil-change model are those that make up the *educational process*; that is, all the activities in the school expressly designed to bring about changes for the better in pupils: lessons in arithmetic, recreational activities, consultation with parents, vocational counseling, etc. Three principal questions are to be asked about the educational processes in any school: (1) Are they adapted to the individual needs of the children in the school? (2) Do they work, that is, do they tend to change pupils in *desirable* ways? and (3) What, if any, negative side effects may they be having on the growth of the children?

The four sets of variables just described—input, output, surrounding conditions, and educational process—interact with one another in complex ways. That is, the pupil output variables are affected by all the other variables. Similarly, the educational process variables are influenced by both the pupil input and the surrounding conditions. And certain of the surrounding conditions may be influenced by certain of the educational processes. This last could happen, for instance, if a school embarked on a cooperative work-study program with businesses in its enrollment area.

From the foregoing considerations, it is clear that if a school staff is to maximize pupil output in any particular way, it must be aware of the nature of the interactions among the variables in the system and be given sufficient information to cope with them in its work. This in turn means that, insofar as possible, all variables in the system must be measured and appropriately interrelated and combined to produce readily interpretable indices by which the staff can know how much its own efforts are producing hoped-for changes in pupils, after making due allowance for those variables over which it has little or no control. I call such indices *school effectiveness indices* (SEI's). They are the means whereby a school staff may be held responsible for *knowing* how well it is doing.

The functioning of a school can be described by a profile of school effectiveness indices, so that each school staff can readily locate the points at which its educational program is strong or weak. Such a profile is fundamentally different from the traditional test-score profile, which is ordinarily generated from the grade equivalencies attached to the general run of standardized achievement tests. The underlying rationale of an SEI profile rejects grade equivalencies as essentially meaningless numbers that tend to be grossly misleading as indicators of a school's effectiveness. Appropriate indices in the SEI profile of any given school at any given level can be derived only through a procedure involving *all* the schools at the same level in the district. The procedure consists of a series of regression analyses which I shall touch upon presently.

Two features of an SEI profile differentiate it from the usual test-score profile. First, each index summarizes how effective the school has been in promoting one type of pupil development over a definite span of years; for example, the three years from the beginning of grade four to the end of grade six. Second, the profile has two dimensions: a pupil development dimension comprehending different areas of pupil growth (e.g., growth in self-esteem, growth in the basic skills, growth in social behavior) and a level-of-pupil-input dimension which might encompass three categories of children in accordance with their varying levels of development in any area at the time they entered grade four.

With this sort of profile it should be possible to discern in which areas of pupil development a school is more or less effective with different groups of pupils. Thus, an SEI profile for a grade four-to-six school should be capable of answering questions like the following: In its teaching of reading over the three-year period, has the school done a better or worse job with pupils who entered grade four with a low level of reading performance as compared with those who entered with a high level of reading performance? During the three-year period, has the school been more or less effective in developing children's number skills than in developing their sense of self-esteem, or their social behavior, or their health habits?

The areas of pupil development to be incorporated in the educational accounting system for any district must grow out of an earnest effort to reach agreement among all the parties involved (teachers, administrators, board members, parents, pupils) concerning the pupil performance objectives that are to be sought. Such objectives will vary for schools encompassing different grade levels, and they will also vary, in accordance with local needs, among schools serving any given grade levels.

Securing agreement on the objectives is no mean enterprise, but it is obviously fundamental to a meaningful approach to the establishment of any basis for holding professional educators accountable for their own performance in the schools.

One important point to keep in mind about any school effectiveness index is that it is a measure that must be *derived* from a large number of more fundamental measures. These more fundamental measures consist of three of the sets of variables suggested earlier in the discussion of the pupil-change model of a school as a social system, namely, (1) the pupil input variables, (2) the *hard-to-change* surrounding conditions, and (3) the pupil output variables. Measures of *easy-to-change* surrounding condition variables and of the educational process variables do not enter into the derivation of SEI's. They become of central importance subsequently in identifying the specific actions a school staff should take to improve the effectiveness of its operations.

The fundamental measures from which the indices are to be derived can take many different forms: academic achievement tests; questionnaires to get at matters like pupil self-esteem; physical examinations to assess health and health habits; a wide range of sociological measures to assess community conditions; and measures of various aspects of the school plant, equipment, and personnel. Techniques for securing many of these measures are already available, but new and more refined ones will be required before a reasonably equitable educational accounting system can be fully operable.

Given the total array of measures required for the derivation of the SEI's, the first step in the derivation will be to apply such measures in all schools in the system at any given level (e.g., all the elementary schools, all the senior high schools) to secure the necessary information on pupil input and on the hard-to-change surrounding conditions.

The second step, to be taken perhaps two or three years later, will be to obtain output measures on the same pupils, i.e., those pupils who have remained in the same schools during the period in question.

The third step will be to distribute the pupils within each school into three groups—high, middle, and low—on each of the input measures. Two points are to be especially noted about this step. First, the distribution of input measures must be "within school" distributions, with the consequence that the pupils constituting the "high" group in one school could conceivably be in the "low" group at another school where the input levels run higher with respect to any particular "area of development." Secondly, within any school, a pupil's input level could be high in one area of development (e.g., basic skills) and middle or low in another area of development (e.g., health).

The fourth step in deriving the SEI's is to compute, for each school, the averages of the hard-to-change condition variables that characterize the environment within which the school has had to operate.

The fifth step is to get, again for each school, the average values of all the output measures for each of the three groups of pupils as identified by the input measures.

When all these data are in hand it becomes possible, by means of a series of regression analyses, to compute the SEI's that form the profile of each school.

A rough impression of how this process works may be obtained from an examination of the chart in Figure 1, which was developed from reading test scores obtained on pupils in ninety-one schools. (It should be noted that this example does not include the important refinement that calls for assessing

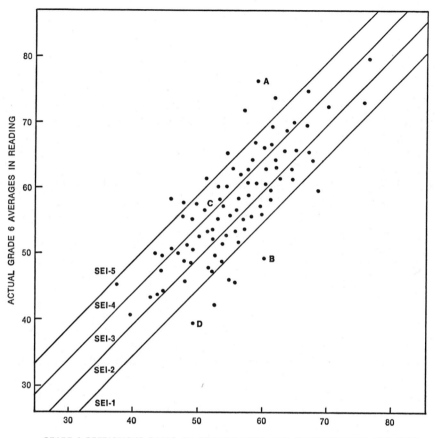

GRADE 6 PREDICTIONS BASED ON GRADE 4 INPUT AND ENVIRONMENTAL VARIABLES

FIGURE 1   **Method of Deriving School Effectiveness Indices
in the Teaching of Reading**

the schools' effectiveness for each of three levels of pupil input in reading.)
The measures of input in reading were taken at the beginning of grade four,
and the measures of output at the end of grade six. The numbers along the
horizontal axis of the chart summarize the level of grade four reading input
and hard-to-change conditions with which each school has had to contend.
This summarization is expressed in terms of the grade six predicted average
reading levels as determined by the regression analysis.

The numbers along the vertical axis show the *actual* average reading levels
for each school at the end of grade six. For each school, the discrepancy between its *predicted* grade six reading level and its *actual* grade six average

reading level is used as the measure of the effectiveness with which it has been teaching reading over the three-year period. It is the discrepancy between predicted and actual level of performance that is used to determine the SEI in reading for any school. In this case the SEI's have been assigned arbitrary values ranging from a low of one to a high of five.

Consider the two schools A and B. They both have predicted grade six reading averages of about 60. This indicates that they can be deemed to have been operating in situations that are equivalent in respect to their levels of input at grade four and the hard-to-change conditions that have obtained over the three-year period during which their pupils have gone from grades four through six.

The actual reading output levels at grade six for schools A and B are considerably different. A's actual level is about 73; B's actual level is about 48. As a consequence, school A gets an effectiveness index for the teaching of reading of five, while school B gets an effectiveness index of only one.

Schools C and D present a similar picture, but at a lower level of pupil input and hard-to-change conditions. Both have predicted averages of about 50, but C's actual average is about 56, while D's is only 38. Therefore C gets an SEI of four, and D gets an SEI of only one.

From these two pairs of illustrations, it should be noted that the proposed method of computing school effectiveness indices *automatically* adjusts for the differing circumstances in which schools must operate. This feature of the index is a *sine qua non* of any system by which school staffs are to be held professionally accountable.

It was suggested at the beginning of this paper that one of the general principles underlying the concept of professional accountability is that the staff of a school is to be held responsible for *using* its knowledge of where the school stands with respect to the intellectual and personal-social development of its pupils. This is to say that it is not sufficient for a school to "render an accounting" of its educational effectiveness. If the accounting is to have any educational payoff for the pupils whom the school is supposed to serve, the indices should point to some specific corrective actions designed to increase the school's effectiveness.

Many of such actions will perforce be outside the scope of the school itself, and responsibility for taking them must rest with the central administration. In most cases, however, a considerable number of such corrective actions should be well within the competence of the professional staff of the individual school. Responsibility for carrying them out can and should rest with that staff.

The function of school effectiveness indices in this connection is to indicate where a school staff might turn to find ways of improving its performance.

To illustrate how the SEI's might serve this purpose, let us speculate further about the relative positions of schools A and B in Figure 1. Since both schools show the same *predicted* output in reading for such pupils, it can be presumed that both schools are operating under equivalent advantages and handicaps in respect to the conditions that affect the reading ability of those pupils. Therefore, it is entirely legitimate to raise the questions: Why is school A doing so much better than school B in the teaching of reading? What specifically is school A doing for its pupils that school B is not now doing, but presumably *could* be doing and *ought* to be doing to close the gap between them?

The reasons for the discrepancy between the two schools on this particular SEI are to be sought among the two sets of variables that did not enter into the derivation of the SEI's: namely, those variables that were designated "educational process" and those designated "easy-to-change surrounding conditions." A systematic comparison of how the two schools stand with respect to these variables should provide the professional staff of school B with useful clues for actions that might be taken to increase its effectiveness in the teaching of reading.

The outcome of this exercise might turn up something like this:

1. School A conducts an intensive summer program in reading; school B does not.
2. School A has a tutorial program conducted by high school students for any pupil who wishes to improve his reading; school B has no such program.
3. School A conducts parent-teacher study groups to stimulate more reading in the home; school B has little contact of any kind with the parents of its pupils.

There is, of course, no absolute guarantee that if school B were to initiate such programs it would automatically raise its SEI in reading from one to five. The factors involved in the life and workings of a school are not all that certain and clear-cut. Nevertheless, there should be a plain obligation on the staff of school B to at least *try* the procedures that appear to be working for school A and to monitor such efforts over a sufficient period to see whether they are having the desired effects. This particularization of staff effort contains the essence of what must be involved in any attempt to guarantee the professional accountability of a school staff.

The approach to accountability through a system of SEI's, if it is well understood and accepted throughout the schools of the district, should provide a mechanism for stimulating directed professional efforts toward the continuous improvement of educational practice on many fronts in all the schools.

Plans and Cautions

Clearly a full-scale educational accounting system of the sort here envisaged is hardly one that can be designed and installed full-blown in a year or two. It is one that would have to be worked out, piece by piece, over a considerable period of years. It contains technical problems many of which cannot be foreseen in advance and can only be tackled as the accounting system comes into actual operation. More importantly, it would require a massive effort to secure the necessary understanding and cooperation from all the professional and community groups to be affected by it.

Nevertheless, because of the urgency of the situation in urban education and because no adequate and equitable educational accounting system can ever eventuate until some practical action is taken to get it under way, it is strongly suggested that a beginning should be made forthwith by means of a two-pronged approach. One approach would look to the carrying out of a *partial* short-range plan over the next two years; the other to the laying out of a long-range plan for the full-scale operation of the system to be achieved in say, six years.

The *short-range plan* could begin with the reasonable assumption that there are two areas of pupil development that are of universal concern, especially as they touch the lives of minority group children in the early years of their schooling. These areas are reading and health. Acting on this assumption, one might, from currently available data, obtain input measures of these two variables on all children entering grades one and three with a view to getting output measures on the same children two years later. During the two intervening years a number of the more readily available measures of the hard-to-change conditions affecting each of the elementary schools in the system could conceivably be obtained, e.g., socioeconomic status of pupils' parents, population density and ethnicity of each enrollment area, pupil-teacher ratio, classroom and playground footage per pupil, rate of pupil mobility, and the like. Thus, by the end of the second year, one would be in a position to compute tentative school effectiveness indices and prepare two SEI profiles for each elementary school in the system—one covering grades one and two, the other covering grades three and four. These profiles could then be used as bases for local discussions concerning their meaning and utility as measures of professional accountability. (As rapidly as community acceptance was achieved, the system could be put on an annual basis and enlarged year by year to include more grades and more areas of pupil development.)

The purpose of a short-range program of this sort would be twofold: (1) to provide a first approximation of two important and practically useful objective criteria of professional accountability, and (2) to provide a concrete basis for bringing about a genuine understanding of what an educational accounting system is and how it can work for the benefit of the schools and the children who attend them.

Concurrently with the foregoing short-range effort, the development of a *long-range plan* should get under way. The first step in this planning process would be to initiate parent-teacher discussions to try (1) to reach a consensus on educational objectives in terms of the areas of pupil development that should be involved in an overall annual system for professional accounting, and (2) to agree on the priorities among such objectives as they might most appropriately apply to the educational needs of the pupils in each school. The second step in the long-range plan would be to assemble instruments for measuring input and output which would be appropriate and compatible with the objectives for each level of schooling. The third step would be to work out the means for collecting and analyzing the necessary data for measuring the conditions within which each school is operating and the specific processes that characterize its operations.

One reason for initiating long-range planning concurrently with working through a partial short-range program is to try to ensure that the ultimate goal of the full-scale system will not be lost from sight while major attention is necessarily focused on the detailed problems of getting a partial operating system under way quickly. In the search for ways around the short-range problems, it is altogether probable that a number of compromises will have to be made. The danger is that, unless the final end is kept in full view, some of these compromises will be such as to preclude attainment of a viable total system.

One mistake, for instance, that could be made at the outset of the short-range program would be to yield to demands to use the input or output measures as if they were themselves measures of school effectiveness. The whole point of this paper is that a meaningful and equitable accounting of school effectiveness is possible *only* under two stringent conditions: (1) it must rest on at least two measures of pupil performance with a sufficient interval between them—probably not less than two years—to permit the school to have an effect on pupil learning which is large enough to be observable; and (2) any output measure of pupil performance must be read in light of the level of pupil input and also in light of the conditions in which the school has been forced to operate during the period for which its effectiveness in the several areas of pupil development is being indexed. This point cannot be too strongly stressed. To compromise with this basic principle would wreck the entire enterprise.

A second mistake that could seriously damage the development of the system would be to introduce into it measures of I.Q. as though they were measures of pupil input available simultaneously with measures of pupil output. This type of misuse of test scores has had a disastrous effect on the interpretation of educational measurements for at least fifty years. It should not be prolonged.

A third type of mistake to be avoided is that of concentrating the effort to develop SEI's on a certain *selected* group of schools (e.g., those in poverty areas) but not on others. If this is done the SEI's simply will not mean anything. A basic requirement in their derivation and use is that the essential measures must be obtained on *all* schools in the system so as to determine which schools are indeed comparable.

One other type of mistake that could be made in embarking on the short-range project would be to concentrate all the effort on a single area of pupil development, namely, the "basic skills." The danger here—and it is one by which schools have all too frequently been trapped—is threefold. First, it encourages the notion that, as far as the school is concerned, training in the basic skills is all that matters in a society where so many other human characteristics also matter. Secondly, it tends toward neglect of the fact that if a school gives exclusive attention to this one area of pupil development, it may purchase success in this area at the expense of failure in other areas—social behavior, for instance. Thirdly, it tends to blind people to the interrelatedness of educational objectives, that is, to the fact that pupil development in one area may be heavily dependent on development in other areas. Learning to read, for example, may be dependent on the pupil's maintaining good health. And the pupil's sense of his worth as a human being may be dependent on his ability to read. It is for these reasons that the short-range program suggested above includes at a minimum two widely different areas of pupil development.

The term *educational accountability*, as used most recently by certain economists, systems analysts, and the like, has frequently been based on a conceptualization that tends, by analogy, to equate the educational process with the type of engineering process that applies to industrial production. It is this sort of analogy, for instance, that appears to underlie proposals for "guaranteed performance contracting" as exemplified in the much-publicized Texarkana project. The analogy is useful to a point. But there is also a point beyond which it can be so seriously misleading as to undermine any sensible efforts to develop objective criteria of professional accountability.

It must be constantly kept in mind that the educational process is *not* on all fours with an industrial process; it is a social process in which human beings are continually interacting with other human beings in ways that are imperfectly measurable or predictable. Education does not deal with inert raw materials, but with living minds that are instinctively concerned first with preserving their own integrity and second with reaching a meaningful accommodation with the world around them. The output of the educational process is never a "finished product" whose characteristics can be rigorously specified in advance; it is an individual who is sufficiently aware of his own incompleteness to make him want to keep on growing and learning and trying to solve the riddle of his own existence in a world that neither he nor anyone else can fully understand or predict.

It is for this reason that the problems involved in developing objective criteria of professional accountability will always be hard problems. They are problems, however, that must be tackled with all the human insight and good-will that can be mustered if the schools of this urban society are to meet the large challenges that now confront them.

An Approach to Developing Accountability Measures for the Public Schools

Stephen M. Barro

. . . Accountability in the abstract is a concept to which few would take exception. The doctrine that those employed by the public to provide a service—especially those vested with decsion-making power—should be answerable for their product is one that is accepted readily in other spheres and that many would be willing to extend, in principle, to public education. The problems arise in making the concept operational. Then it becomes necessary to deal with a number of sticky questions: To what extent should each participant in the educational process—teacher, principal, and administrator—be held responsible for results? To whom should they be responsible? How are "results" to be defined and measured? How will each participant's contribution be determined? What will be the consequences for professional educators of being held responsible? These are the substantive issues that need to be treated in a discussion of approaches to implementing the accountability concept. . . .

Dr. Barro is an economist with the Rand Corporation. This article originally appeared in *Phi Delta Kappan* (December 1970). Copyright ©1970 by Phi Delta Kappa, Inc. Abridged and reprinted by permission.

   Proposals for making the schools accountable range from managerial or
quality control improvements within the existing system to professional incentive plans ("merit pay" or performance contracting), to broad restructuring of relationships between educators and clients (community-controlled
schools or voucher-type market solutions). These proposals, though not mutu-
ally exclusive, are quite diverse both with respect to the kinds of restructuring
they would imply and the prospective educational consequences. However,
they are alike in one important respect: Each can be carried out only with
adequate information on the individual and the collective effectiveness of
participants in the educational process. At present, such information does not
exist in school systems. Therefore, a major consideration in moving toward
accountability must be development of information systems, including the
data-gathering and analytical activities needed to support them. This aspect
of accountability—the nature of the required effectiveness indicators and the
means of obtaining them—will be the principal subject of the remainder of
this paper.
   Progress in establishing accountability for results within school systems is
likely to depend directly on success in developing two specific kinds of effectiveness information: (1) improved, more comprehensive pupil performance measurements; and (2) estimates of contributions to measured pupil
performance by individual teachers, administrators, schools, and districts.
As will be seen, the two have very different implications. The first calls primarily for expansion and refinement of what is now done in the measurement
area. The second requires a kind of analysis that is both highly technical and
new to school systems and poses a much greater challenge.
   The need for more extensive pupil performance measurement is evident.
If teachers, for example, are to be held responsible for what is learned by their
pupils, then pupil performance must be measured at least yearly so that gains
associated with each teacher can be identified. Also, if the overall effectiveness
of educators and schools is to be assessed, measurement will have to be extended to many more dimensions of pupil performance than are covered
by instruments in common use. This implies more comprehensive, more frequent testing than is standard practice in most school systems. In the longer
run, it will probably require substantial efforts to develop and validate more
powerful measurement instruments.
   But no program of performance measurement alone, no matter how comprehensive or sophisticated, is sufficient to establish accountability. To do
that, we must also be able to attribute results (performance gains) to sources.
Only by knowing the contributions of individual professionals or schools
would it be possible, for example, for a district to operate an incentive pay or
promotion system; for community boards in a decentralized system to evaluate local schools and their staffs; or for parents, under a voucher system, to

make informed decisions about schools for their children. To emphasize this point, from now on the term "accountability measures" will be used specifically to refer to estimates of contributions to pupil performance by individual agents in the educational process. These are described as "estimates" advisedly, because, unlike performance, which can be measured directly, *contributions* to performance cannot be measured directly but must be *inferred* from comparative analysis of different classrooms, schools, and districts. The analytical methods for determining individual contributions to pupil performance are the heart of the proposed accountability measurement system.

A Proposed Approach

In the following pages we describe a specific approach that could be followed by a school system interested in deriving accountability measures, as they have just been defined. First, a general rationale for the proposed approach is presented. Then the analytical methodology to be used is discussed in more detail.

For what results should educators be held responsible? Ideally, a school system and its constituent parts, as appropriate, should be held responsible for performance in three areas: (1) selecting "correct" objectives and assigning them appropriate priorities, (2) achieving all the stated (or implicit) objectives, and (3) avoiding unintentional adverse effects on pupils. Realistically, much less can even be attempted. The first of the three areas falls entirely outside the realm of objective measurement and analysis, assessment of objectives being an intrinsically subjective, value-laden, and often highly political process. The other two areas can be dealt with in part, subject to the sometimes severe limitations to the current state of the art of educational measurement. The answer to the question posed above must inevitably be a compromise, and not necessarily a favorable one, between what is desirable and what can actually be done.

Any school system aims at affecting many dimensions of pupil performance. In principle, we would like to consider all of them—appropriately weighted—when we assess teacher, school, or district effectiveness. In practice, it is feasible to work with only a subset of educational outcomes, namely, those for which (a) objectives are well defined and (b) we have some ability to measure output. The dimensions of performance that meet these qualifications tend to fall into two groups: first, certain categories of cognitive skills, including reading and mathematics, for which standardized, validated tests are available; second, certain affective dimensions—socialization, attitudes toward the community, self-concept, and the like—for which we have such indicators or proxies as rates of absenteeism, dropout rates, and incidence of vandalism and delinquency. For practical purposes, these are the kinds of educational outcome measures that would be immediately available to a school system setting out today to develop an accountability system.

Because of the limited development of educational measurement, it seems more feasible to pursue this approach to accountability in the elementary grades than at higher levels, at least in the short run. Adequate instruments are available for the basic skill areas, especially reading, which are the targets of most efforts to improve educational quality at the elementary level. They are not generally available and certainly not as widely used or accepted for the subject areas taught in the secondary schools. Presumably, this is partly because measurement in those areas is inherently more difficult; it is partly, also, because there is much less agreement about the objectives of secondary education. Whatever the reason, establishing accountability for results at the secondary level is likely to be more difficult. Pending further progress in specifying objectives and measuring output, experiments with accountability measurement systems would probably be more fruitfully carried on in the elementary schools.

Fortunately, existing shortcomings in the measurement area can be overcome in time. Serious efforts to make accountability a reality should, themselves, spur progress in the measurement field. However, for the benefits of progress to be realized, the system must be "open"—not restricted to certain dimensions of performance. For this reason, the methodology described here has been designed to be in no way limiting with respect to the kinds of outcome measures that can be handled or the number of dimensions that can ultimately be included.

Who should be accountable for what? Once we have determined what kinds of pupil progress to measure, we can turn to the more difficult problem of determining how much teachers, principals, administrators, and others have contributed to the measured results. This is the key element in a methodology for accountability measurement.

The method proposed here rests on the following general principle: *Each participant in the educational process should be held responsible only for those educational outcomes that he can affect by his actions or decisions and only to the extent that he can affect them.* Teachers, for example, should not be deemed "ineffective" because of shortcomings in the curriculum or the way in which instruction is organized, assuming that those matters are determined at the school and district level and not by the individual teacher. The appropriate question is, "How well does the teacher perform, given the environment (possibly adverse) in which she must work and the constraints (possibly overly restrictive) imposed upon her?" Similarly, school principals and other administrators at the school level should be evaluated according to how well they perform within constraints established by the central administration.

The question then arises of how we know the extent to which teachers or administrators can affect outcomes by actions within their own spheres of responsibility. The answer is that we do not know *a priori*; we must find out from the performance data. This leads to a second principle: *The range over which a teacher, a school principal, or an administrator may be expected to affect outcomes is to be determined empirically from analysis of results obtained by all personnel working in comparable circumstances.* Several implications follow from this statement. First, it clearly establishes that the accountability measures will be relative, involving comparisons among educators at each level of the system. Second, it restricts the applicability of the methodology to systems large enough to have a wide range of professional competence at each level and enough observations to permit reliable estimation of the range of potential teacher and school effects. (This does not mean that accountability cannot be established in small school districts. It does mean that the analysis must take place in a broader context, such as a regional or statewide evaluation of performance, which may encompass many districts.) Third, it foreshadows several characteristics of the statistical models needed to infer contributions to results. To bring out the meaning of these principles in more detail, we will explore them from the points of view of teachers, school administrators, and district administrators, respectively.

We know that the educational results obtained in a particular classroom (e.g., pupils' scores on a standard reading test) are determined by many other things besides the skill and effort of the teacher. The analyses in the Coleman report,[1] other analyses of the Coleman survey data,[2] and other statistical studies of the determinants of pupil achievement[3] show that a large fraction of variation in performance levels is accounted for by out-of-school variables, such as the pupils' socioeconomic status and home environment. Another large fraction is attributable to a so-called "peer group" effect; that is, it depends on characteristics of a pupil's classmates rather than on what takes place in the school. Of the fraction of the variation that *is* explained by school variables, only part can be attributed to teachers. Some portion must also be assigned to differences in resource availability at the classroom and school level and differences among schools in the quality of their management and support. Thus, the problem is to separate out the teacher effect from all the others.

To illustrate the implications for the design of an accountability system, consider the problem of comparing teachers who teach very different groups

---

[1]James S. Coleman *et al., Equality of Educational Opportunity* (Washington, D.C.: Office of Education, 1966).

[2]George W. Mayeske *et al.,* "A Study of Our Nation's Schools" (A working paper) (Washington, D.C.: Office of Education, 1970).

[3]Eric A. Hanushek, "The Education of Negroes and Whites" (Ph.D. diss., M.I.T., 1968); and Herbert J. Kiesling, "The Relationship of School Inputs to Public School Performance in New York State," The Rand Corporation, P-4211 (October 1969).

of children. For simplicity, suppose that there are two groups of pupils in a school system, each internally homogeneous, which we may call "middle-class white" and "poor minority." Assume that all nonteacher inputs associated with the schools are identical for the two groups. Then, based on general expierence, we would probably expect the whole distribution of results to be higher for the former group than for the latter. In measuring gain in reading performance, we might well find, for example, that even the poorest teacher of middle-class white children obtains higher average gains in her class than the majority of teachers of poor minority children. Moreover, the ranges over which results vary in the two groups might be unequal.

If we have reason to believe that the teachers associated with the poor minority children are about as good, on the average, as those associated with the middle-class white children—that is, if they are drawn from the same manpower pool and assigned to schools and classrooms without bias—then it is apparent that both the difference in average performance of the two groups of pupils and the difference in the range of performance must be taken into account in assessing each teacher's contribution. A teacher whose class registers gains, say, in the upper 10 percent of all poor minority classes should be considered as effective as one whose middle-class white group scores in the upper 10 percent for that category, even though the absolute performance gain in the latter case will probably be much greater.

This illustrates that accountability measures are relative in two senses. First, they are relative in that each teacher's contribution is evaluated by comparing it with the contributions made by other teachers in similar circumstances. In a large city or state school system, it can safely be assumed that the range of teacher capabilities covers the spectrum from poor to excellent. Therefore, the range of observed outcomes, after differences in circumstances have been allowed for, is likely to be representative of the range over which teacher quality can be expected to influence results, given the existing institutional framework. It may be objected that the range of outcomes presently observed understates the potential range of accomplishment because present classroom methods, curricula, teacher training programs, etc., are not optimal. This may be true and important, but it is not relevant in establishing teacher accountability because the authority to change those aspects of the system does not rest with the teacher.

Second, accountability measures are relative in that pupil characteristics and other nonteacher influences on pupil performance must be taken fully into account in measuring each teacher's contribution. Operationally, this means that statistical analyses will have to be conducted of the effects of such variables as ethnicity, socioeconomic status, and prior educational experience on a pupil's progress in a given classroom. Also, the effects of classroom or school variables other than teacher capabilities will have to be taken into account. Performance levels of the pupils assigned to different teachers can be compared only after measured performance has been adjusted for all of these variables. The statistical model for computing these adjustments is, therefore, the most important element in the accountability measurement system.

Parallel reasoning suggests that school administrators can be held account-able for relative levels of pupil performance in their schools to the extent that the outcomes are not attributable to pupil, teacher, or classroom character-istics or to school variables that they cannot control. The question is, having adjusted for differences in pupil and teacher inputs and having taken account of other characteristics of the schools, are their unexplained differences among schools that can be attributed to differences in the quality of school leadership and administration? Just as for teachers, accountability measures for school administrators are measures of relative pupil performance in a school after adjusting the data for differences in variables outside the administrators' control.

Consideration of the accountability problem at the school level draws attention to one difficulty with the concept of accountability measurement that may also, in some cases, be present at the classroom level. The difficulty is that although we would like to establish accountability for individual profes-sionals, when two or more persons work together to perform an educational task there is no statistical way of separating their effects. This is easy to see at the school level. If a principal and two assistant principals administer a school, we may be able to evaluate their relative proficiency as a team, but since it is not likely that their respective administrative tasks would relate to different pupil performance measures there is no way of judging their individual con-tributions by analyzing educational outcomes. Similarly, if a classroom teacher works with a teaching assistant, there is no way, strictly speaking, to separate the contributions of the two. It is conventional in these situations to say that the senior person, who has supervisory authority, bears the responsibility for results. However, while this is administratively and perhaps even legally valid, it provides no solution to the problem of assessing the effort and skills of indi-viduals. Therefore, there are definite limits, which must be kept in mind, to the capacity of a statistically based accountability system to aid in assessing individual proficiency.

Although the same approach applies, in principle, to comparisons among districts (or decentralized components of larger districts), there are problems that may limit its usefulness in establishing accountability at the district level. One, of course, is the problem that has just been alluded to. Even if it were possible to establish the existence of overall district effects, it would be impos-sible to isolate the contributions of the local district board, the district super-intendent, and other members of the district staff. A second problem is that comparisons among districts can easily fail to take account of intangible community characteristics that may affect school performance. For example, such factors as community cohesion, political attitudes, and the existence of racial or other intergroup tensions could strongly influence the whole tone of education. It would be very difficult to separate effects of these factors from effects of direct, district-related variables in trying to assess overall district performance. Third, the concept of responsibility at the district level needs clarifying. In comparing schools, for example, it seems reasonable to adjust for differences in teacher characteristics on the grounds that school administrators should be evaluated according to how well they do, given the personnel assigned to them. However, at the district level, personnel selection itself is one of the functions for which administrators must be held accountable, as are resource allocation, program design, choice of curriculum, and other factors that appear as "givens" to the schools. In other words, in assessing comparative district performance, very little about districts can properly be considered as externally determined except, perhaps, the total level of available resources. In addition, of course, there are constraints imposed by state or federal authorities, but these are likely to be the same across districts. The appropriate policy, then, seems to be to include district identity as a variable in comparing schools and teachers so that net district effects, if any, will be taken into account. Districts themselves should be compared on a different basis, allowing only for differences in pupil characteristics, community variables, and overall constraints that are truly outside district control.

A Proposed Methodology

The basic analytical problem in accountability measurement is to develop a technique for estimating the contributions to pupil performance of individual agents in the educational process. A statistical method that may be suitable for that purpose is described here. The basic technique is multiple regression analysis of the relationship between pupil performance and an array of pupil, teacher, and school characteristics. However, the proposed method calls for two or three separate stages of analysis. The strategy is first to estimate the amount of performance variation that exists among classrooms after pupil characteristics have been taken into account, then, in subsequent stages, to attempt to attribute the interclassroom differences to teachers, other classroom variables, and school characteristics. This methodology applies both to large school districts, within which it is suitable for estimating the relative effectiveness of individual teachers and schools in advancing pupil performance, and to state school systems, where it can be used, in addition, to obtain estimates of the relative effectiveness of districts. However, as noted above, there are problems that may limit its utility at the interdistrict level.

Since we are interested in estimating the contributions of individual teachers and schools, it is appropriate to use a "value-added" concept of output. That is, the appropriate pupil performance magnitudes to associate with a particular teacher are the *gains* in performance made by pupils while in her class. Ideally, the output data would be generated by a program of annual (or more frequent) performance measurement, which would automatically provide before and after measures for pupils at each grade level.

It is assumed that a number of dimensions of pupil performance will be measured, some by standardized tests and some by other indicators or proxy variables. Specific measurement instruments to be used and dimensions of performance to be measured would have to be determined by individual school systems in accordance with their educational objectives. Almost every school system will be likely to include reading achievement scores and other scores on standardized tests of cognitive skills among its output variables. Also, it will generally be desirable to include attendance or absenteeism as a variable, both because it may be a proxy for various attitudinal output variables and because it may be an important variable to use in explaining performance. Otherwise, there are innumerable possibilities for dealing with additional dimensions of cognitive and affective performance. The methodology is intended to apply to any dimension of performance that can be quantified at least on an ordinal scale. Therefore, within a very broad range, it is not affected by the choice of output measures by a potential user.

To conform with the model to be described below, the variables entering into the analysis are classified according to the following taxonomy:

1. Individual pupil characteristics (ethnicity, socioeconomic status, home, family, and neighborhood characteristics, age, prior performance, etc.).
2. Teacher and classroom characteristics.
   (a) Group characteristics of the pupils (ethnic and socioeconomic composition, distribution of prior performance levels, etc., within the classroom).
   (b) Teacher characteristics (age, training, experience, ability and personality measures if available, ethnic and socioeconomic background, etc.).
   (c) Other classroom characteristics (measures of resource availability: class size, amount of instructional support, amount of materials, condition of physical facilities, etc.).
3. School characteristics.
   (a) Group characteristics of the pupils (same as 2a, but based on the pupil population of the whole school).
   (b) Staff characteristics (averages of characteristics in 2b for the school as a whole, turnover and transfer rates; characteristics of administrators—same as 2b).

(c) Other school characteristics (measures of resource availability: age and condition of building, availability of facilities, amount of administrative and support staff, etc.).

No attempt will be made to specify precisely what items should be collected under each of the above headings. Determination of the actual set of variables to be used in a school system would have to follow preliminary experimentation, examination of existing data, and an investigation of the feasibility, difficulty, and cost of obtaining various kinds of information.

The first step is to determine how different pupil performance in each classroom at a given grade level is from mean performance in all classrooms, *after* differences in individual pupil characteristics have been allowed for. The procedure consists of performing a multiple regression analysis with gain in pupil performance as the dependent variable. The independent variables would include (a) the individual pupil characteristics (category 1 of the taxonomy), and (b) a set of "dummy" variables, or identifiers, one for each classroom in the sample. The latter would permit direct estimation of the degree to which pupil performance in each classroom differs from pupil performance in the average classroom. Thus, the product of the first stage of the analysis would be a set of estimates of individual classroom effects, each of which represents the combined effect on pupil performance in a classroom of all the classroom and school variables included in categories 2 and 3 of the taxonomy. At the same time, the procedure would automatically provide measures of the accuracy with which each classroom effect has been estimated. Therefore, it would be possible to say whether average performance gains in a particular classroom are significantly higher or lower than would be expected in a "typical" classroom or not significantly different from the mean.

Heuristically, this procedure compares performance gains by pupils in a classroom with gains that comparable pupils would be likely to achieve in a hypothetical "average" classroom of the system. This can be thought of as comparison of class performance gains against a norm, except that there is, in effect, a particular norm for each classroom based on its unique set of pupil characteristics. It may also be feasible to carry out the same analysis for specific subgroups of pupils in each class so as to determine, for example, whether there are different classroom effects for children from different ethnic or socioeconomic groups.

The second stage of the analysis has two purposes: (1) to separate the effects of the teacher from effects of nonteacher factors that vary among classrooms; and (2) to determine the extent to which pupil performance can be related to specific, measurable teacher attributes. Again, the method to be used is regression analysis, but in this case with a sample of classroom observations rather than individual pupil observations. The dependent variable is now the classroom effect estimated in stage one. The independent variables are the teacher-classroom characteristics and "dummy" variables distinguishing the individual schools.

Two kinds of information can be obtained from the resulting equations. First, it is possible to find out what fraction of the variation in performance gains among classrooms is accounted for by nonteacher characteristics, including group characteristics of the pupils and measures of resource availability in the classroom. The remaining interclassroom differences provide upper-bound estimates of the effects that can be attributed to teachers. If there is sufficient confidence that the important nonteacher variables have been taken into account, then these estimates provide the best teacher accountability measures. They encompass the effects of both measured and unmeasured teacher characteristics on teacher performance. However, there is some danger that such measures also include effects of group and classroom characteristics that were inadvertently neglected in the analysis and that are not properly attributable to teachers. This problem is referred to again below.

Second, we can find out the extent to which differences among classrooms are explained by measured teacher characteristics. Ideally, of course, we would like to be able to attribute the whole "teacher portion" of performance variation to specific teacher attributes and, having done so, we would be much more confident about our overall estimates of teacher effectiveness. But experience to date with achievement determinant studies has shown that the more readily available teacher characteristics—age, training, experience, and the like—account for only a small fraction of the observed variance. It has been shown that more of the variation can be accounted for when a measure of teacher verbal ability is included.[4] Still more, presumably, could be accounted for if a greater variety of teacher ability and personality measurements were available. At present, however, knowledge of what teacher characteristics influence pupil performance is incomplete, and satisfactory instruments exist for measuring only a limited range of teacher-related variables. This means that with an accountability information system based on current knowledge, the excluded teacher characteristics could be at least as important as those included in determining teacher effectiveness. For the time being, then, the interclassroom variation in results that remains after nonteacher effects have been allowed for probably provides the most useful accountability measures, though the danger of bias due to failure to include all relevant non-teacher characteristics must be recognized.

The principal use of these estimates would be in assessing the relative effectiveness of individual teachers in contributing to gains in pupil performance. More precisely, it would be possible to determine whether each teacher's esti-

[4]Eric A. Hanushek, *The Value of Teachers in Teaching* (Santa Monica, Calif.: The Rand Corporation, 1970).

mated contribution is significantly greater or significantly smaller than that of the average teacher. At least initially, until there is strong confirmation of the validity of the procedure, a rather stringent significance criterion should be used in making these judgments and no attempt should be made to use the results to develop finer gradations of teacher proficiency.

The analysis will also make it possible to determine the extent to which measured teacher characteristics are significantly correlated with teacher effectiveness. Potentially, such information could have important policy implications and impacts on school management, resource allocation, and personnel practices. A number of these potential applications are noted at the end of the paper.

The same analytical techniques can be used in estimating the relative effectiveness of different schools in promoting pupil performance. Conceptually, a school accountability index should measure the difference between pupil performance in an individual school and average pupil performance in all schools after all pupil, teacher, and classroom variables have been accounted for. Such measures can be obtained directly if school dummy variables are included in the regression equation, as described earlier. Of course, the results measure *total* school effects, without distinguishing among effects due to school administration, effects of physical attributes of the school, and effects of characteristics of the pupil population. It may be feasible to perform a third-stage analysis in which the results are systematically adjusted for differences in the latter two categories of variables, leaving residual effects that can be attributed to the school administrators. These would constitute the accountability measures to be used in assessing the effectiveness of the principal and his staff. The results may have policy implications with respect to differential allocation of funds or resources among the different schools and, of course, implications with respect to personnel. Also, as would be done for teachers, an attempt could be made to relate measured characteristics of the school administrators to the estimated school effects. By so doing, it might be possible to learn whether administrator training and experience and other attributes are reflected in measured school output. Even negative results could provide important guidance to research on administrator selection and assignment.

For reasons that have already been stated, it would probably be desirable to treat comparisons among districts separately from comparisons among classrooms and schools. This could be done by means of yet another regression analysis, with individual pupil performance gain as the dependent variable and with independent variables consisting of pupil and community characteristics, measures of resource availability, and a dummy variable or identifier for each district being compared. The purpose would be to determine whether there are significant differences in results among districts once the other factors have been allowed for. If there are, the findings could be interpreted as reflections of differences in the quality of district policy making and management. But as pointed out earlier, there would be uncertainty as to the causes of either shortcomings or superior performance. Nevertheless, the results could have some important, policy-related uses, as will be noted shortly.

The Need for Experimental
Verification of the Approach

The methodology described here carries no guarantee. Its success in relating outcomes to sources may depend both on features of the school systems to which it is applied and on the adequacy of the statistical models in mirroring the underlying (and unknown) input-output relationships in education. The validity and usefulness of the results must be determined empirically from field testing in actual school systems. Experimental verification, possibly requiring several cycles of refinement and testing, must precede implementation of a "working" accountability system.

Three kinds of technical problems can threaten the validity of the system: intercorrelation, omission of variables, and structural limitations of the models. None of these can be discussed in detail without mathematics. However, a brief explanation of each is offered so that the outlook for the proposed approach can be realistically assessed.

This is a problem that may arise where there are processes in a school system that create associations (correlations) between supposedly independent variables in the model. An important example is the process, said to exist in many systems, whereby more experienced, better trained, or simply "better" teachers tend to be assigned or transferred to schools with higher socioeconomic status (SES) pupils. Where this occurs, pupil SES will be positively correlated with those teacher characteristics. On the average, high SES children would be taught by one kind of teacher, low SES children by another. This would make it difficult to say whether the higher performance gains likely to be observed for high SES pupils are due to their more advantaged backgrounds or to the superior characteristics of their instructors. There would be ambiguity as to the magnitude of the teacher contribution and a corresponding reduction in the reliability of estimates of individual teacher effectiveness. Thus, the quality of accountability information would be impaired.

This problem can take many forms. There may be strong correlations between characteristics of pupils and characteristics of school staffs, between teacher characteristics and non-teacher attributes of the schools, between classroom-level and district-level variables, and so on. The general effect is the same in each instance: ambiguity resulting in diminished ability to attribute results to sources. The existence of this type of ambiguity in analyses of the Coleman survey data is one of the principal findings reported by Mayeske.[5]

There are several things that can be done to mitigate the effects of intercorrelation. One is to stratify the data. For example, if teacher characteristics were linked to pupil SES, it would be possible to stratify the classrooms by pupil SES and to perform separate analyses for each stratum. This would eliminate some of the ambiguity *within* strata. On the other hand, comparisons of teachers *across* strata would be precluded. Another possible solution would be to take account of interdependence explicitly in the statistical models. Some attempts along this line have been made in studies of determinants of school performance. However, this solution is likely to raise a whole new array of technical problems as well as questions about the feasibility of routine use of the methodology within school systems.

The validity and fairness of the proposed approach would depend very strongly on inclusion of all major relevant variables that could plausibly be cited by teachers or administrators to "explain" lower-than-average estimated contributions. This means that all variables would have to be included that (a) have significant, independent effects on performance and (b) are likely to be nonuniformly distributed among classrooms and schools.

It will never be possible to demonstrate in a positive sense that all relevant variables have been included. Many intangible, difficult-to-measure variables, such as pupil attitudes, morale, "classroom climate," etc., can always be suggested. What can be done is to determine as well as possible that none of the additional suggested variables is systematically related to the estimated teacher and school contributions. In an experimental setting, administrators could be interviewed for the purpose of identifying alleged special circumstances, and tests could be carried out to see whether they are systematically related to performance differences.

The models described here may be too simple to take account of some of the important relationships among school inputs and outputs. One such shortcoming has already been noted: The models do not allow for possible interdependencies among the various pupil and school characteristics. Another, which may prove to be more troubling, is that interactions among the various output or performance variables have also not been taken into account.

Researchers have pointed to two distinct kinds of relationships. First, there may be trade-offs between performance areas. A teacher or school may do well in one area partly at the expense of another by allocating resources or time disproportionately between the two. Second, there may be complementary relationships. Increased performance in one area (reading, for ex-

[5]Mayeske, *op. cit.*

ample) may contribute directly to increased performance in others (social studies or mathematics). Therefore, treatment of one dimension of output at a time, without taking the interactions into account, could produce misleading results.

Econometricians have developed "simultaneous" models, consisting of whole sets of equations, specifically to take account of complex, multiple relationships among variables. Some attempts have been made to apply these models to studies of determinants of educational outcomes. It may prove necessary or desirable to use them in an accountability measurement system, despite the complexity they would add, to eliminate biases of simpler models.

Another important reason for thoroughly testing the accountability measurement system is that its validity needs to be assessed. Some of the procedures mentioned above contribute to this end, but more general demonstration would also be desirable. Two procedures that may be feasible in an experimental situation are as follows:

A strong test of whether the method really gets at differences in effectiveness instead of differences in circumstances would be to apply it to the same teachers and schools during two or more years. Consistency in results from year to year would strongly support the methodology. Lack of consistency would show that major influences on performance remained unmeasured or neglected. Certainly, if the results were to be used in any way in connection with personnel assignment, reward, or promotion, the use of several years' estimates would be an important guarantee of both consistency and fairness.

The most direct way to test the validity of the statistical approach is to compare the results with alternative measures of teacher and school effectiveness. The only measures that are likely to be obtainable are subjective assessments by informed and interested parties. Though such evaluations have many shortcomings, it could be valuable in an experimental situation to see how well they agreed with the statistical results. Two important questions that would have to be answered in making such a comparison are: (1) Who are the appropriate raters—peers, administrators, parents, or even pupils? (2) What evaluation instruments could be used to assure that subjective assessments apply to the same dimensions of performance as were taken into account in the statistical analysis? It may not be possible to provide satisfactory answers. Nevertheless, the feasibility of a comparison with direct assessments should be considered in connection with any effort to test the proposed accountability measurement system.

Potential Uses of Accountability Measures

Space does not permit a full review of the potential uses of an accountability measurement system. However, an idea of the range of applications and their utility can be conveyed by listing some of the main possibilities.

The most rudimentary use of the proposed accountability measures is as an identification device. Once relative school effectiveness is known, a variety of actions can follow, even if there is ambiguity about causes. As examples, less formal evaluation efforts can be more precisely targeted once school effectiveness with different kinds of children is known and campaigns can be initiated to discover, disseminate, and emulate good practices of high-performing schools.

Accountability measures may help to improve both staff utilization and selection of new personnel. Personnel utilization could be improved by using information on teacher effectiveness in different spheres and with different types of students for guidance in staff assignment. Selection and recruitment could be aided by using information from the models as a guide to performance-related characteristics of applicants and as a basis for revising selection procedures and criteria.

An accountability measurement system can be used to establish a connection between personnel compensation and performance. One use would be in providing evidence to support inclusion of more relevant variables in pay scales than the universally used and widely criticized training and experience factors. Another possibility would be to use accountability measures as inputs in operating incentive pay or promotion systems. The latter, of course, is a controversial proposal, long resisted by professional organizations. Nevertheless, putting aside other arguments pro and con, the availability of objective measures of individual contributions would eliminate a major objection to economic incentives and help to make the idea more acceptable to all concerned.

An accountability measurement system could also contribute to other aspects of resource allocation in school systems. Analytical results from the models could be of value, for example, in setting policies on class size, supporting services, and similar resource variables. More directly, school accountability measures could provide guidance to district administrators in allocating resources differentially among schools according to educational need. Similarly, state-level results could be used in determining appropriate allocations of state aid funds to districts.

Models developed for accountability could prove to be valuable tools for program evaluation and research. They could be readily adapted for comparing alternative ongoing programs simply by including "program" as one of the classroom variables. Also, "norms" provided by the models for specific types of pupils could be used as reference standards in evaluating experimental programs. This would be preferable, in some cases, to using experimental control groups. Viewed as research tools, the models could help to shed light on one of the most basic, policy-related problems in education, the relationship between school inputs and educational output. The process of developing the models could itself be very instructive. The results could add substantially to our knowledge of how teachers and schools make a difference to their pupils.

In sum, there are many potential uses of the proposed measures and models, some going well beyond what is generally understood by "accountability." If the development of a system is undertaken and carried through to completion, the by-products alone may well prove to be worth the effort.

Accountability in Education

Felix M. Lopez

Accountability refers to the process of expecting each member of an organization to answer to someone for doing specific things according to specific plans and against certain timetables to accomplish tangible performance results. It assumes that everyone who joins an organization does so presumably to help in the achievement of its purposes; it assumes that individual behavior which contributes to these purposes is functional and that which does not is dysfunctional. Accountability is intended, therefore, to insure that the behavior of every member of an organization is largely functional.

Accountability is to be distinguished from responsibility by the fact that the latter is an essential component of authority which cannot be delegated. It is the responsibility of a board of education to insure the effective education of the children in its community. Board members cannot pass this responsibility on to principals and to teachers. But they can hold teachers and principals accountable for the achievement of tangible educational effects *provided* they define clearly what effects they expect and furnish the resources needed to achieve them.

Dr. Lopez is president of Impart, Inc., a division of Behavioral Technology, Inc., New York, N.Y. This article originally appeared in *Phi Delta Kappan* (December 1970). Copyright © 1970 by Phi Delta Kappa, Inc. Reprinted by permission.

Reasons for Failure

A review of accountability programs underlines its uneven, trial-and-error progress and its current inadequacies. Initiated when psychometric theory was largely underdeveloped, embedded early in unrealistic management and legislative mandates, imposed usually from above on unwilling and uncomprehending supervisors, the program has struggled with the common conception that it is an end rather than a means and with an administrative naiveté that treats it as a student's report card. Personnel textbooks have stressed the idea that an accountability plan must be characterized by simplicity, flexibility, and economy. Ignoring the fact that these qualities are not wholly compatible, administrators have attempted to develop programs along these lines. Their inevitable failures have led to the current disillusionment and distrust and, in some quarters, to the belief that the establishment of an effective program is impossible. Nevertheless, a careful examination of efforts to establish accountability programs suggests some underlying misconceptions that explain the many failures.

1. Most accountability programs have been installed in organizational settings that lack the necessary background and organizational traditions to assimilate them. Insufficient emphasis has been placed on the development of an organizational philosophy and on the determination of accountability policies before the implementation of the program.

2. The administrative procedures governing the program have not been attuned to its purposes. There has been a tendency to make the program accomplish a great deal with an oversimplified procedure. The evidence strongly suggests that despite the ardent wish for economy and simplicity, only a program designed for a specific purpose or involving a multimethod approach is likely to succeed.

3. Accountability systems have not been designed to gain acceptance by those who are covered by them nor by those who have to implement them. For the most part, they have been designed by specialists, approved at the highest levels, and imposed without explanation on those who have to implement them. This occurs because the problem is approached from an organizational rather than an individual perspective.

4. The measures of accountability so far developed have not met even minimum standards of reliability and relevancy. This failure is known as the "criterion problem" and can be summarized briefly as follows:

(a) Criteria of effectiveness in a position generally lack clear specifications.
(b) Objective measures, when examined closely, are usually found to be either nonobjective or irrelevant.
(c) Subjective measures, when examined closely, are usually found to be biased or unreliable.

(d) Seemingly adequate criteria can vary over time.

(e) Position effectiveness is really multidimensional: Effectiveness in one aspect of a position does not necessarily mean effectiveness in other aspects.

(f) When effectiveness in different aspects of a position is measured, there is no sure way to combine these measures into a single index of effectiveness.

(g) Different performance patterns achieve the same degree of effectiveness in the same job.

To be successful, therefore, the accountability program must meet the following requirements:

1. It must be an important communications medium in a responsive environment through which members are informed of what is to be accomplished, by whom, and how; wide participation in the obtainment of organization goals must be invited; and the attention of top management must be focused on the accomplishment of individual employees' personal goals.

2. It must reflect an organizational philosophy that inspires confidence and trust in all the members.

3. It must be based on ethical principles and sound policies that can be implemented by a set of dynamic, flexible, and realistic standards, procedures, and practices.

4. It must clearly specify its purposes so that standards, procedures, and practices can be conformed to them.

5. It must be designed primarily to improve the performance of each member in his current job duties. Other effects, such as the acquisition of information on which to base salary and promotion decisions and the personal development of the employees' capacities, may accompany the main effect of improved job performance, but these must be considered merely by-products of the main process.

6. The manner in which the supervisor discusses his evaluation with the subordinate constitutes the core of the process. If this is handled poorly, the program, no matter how well designed and implemented, will fail.

7. To be effective and accepted, both those who use it and those who will be judged by it must participate in the design, installation, administration, and review of the total accountability system.

These principles, then, outline the dimensions of an approach to the establishment of accountability in education. The approach encompasses three broad interventions into the current system, each aimed initially at a distinct level of the organization structure: the top, the middle, and the base, the last named being the teachers themselves. Ultimately, however, all three levels will be involved in all three phases of the accountability program.

Intervention at the Top

Basically, intervention at the top consists of the establishment of organizational goals by the use of a technique referred to in private industry as "Management by Objectives" (MBO) and in government as the "Planning, Programming, and Budgeting System" (PPBS). Since there are many excellent books describing these techniques in detail, we shall confine ourselves here to a brief summary of the method.

The underlying concept of the goal-setting approach is simple: The clearer the idea you have of what you want to accomplish, the greater your chance of accomplishing it. Goal setting, therefore, represents an effort on the part of the management to inhibit the natural tendency of organizational procedures to obscure organizational purposes in the utilization of resources. The central idea is to establish a set of goals for the organization, to integrate individual performance with them, and to relate the rewards system to their accomplishment.

While there is general agreement that this method represents the surest approach to effective management, there is no primrose path to its practical implementation.

In its most commonly accepted form, MBO constitutes an orderly way of goal setting at the top, communication of these goals to lower-unit managers, the development of lower-unit goals that are phased into those set by the higher levels, and comparison of results in terms of goals. The program operates within a network of consultative interviews between supervisor and subordinate in which the subordinate receives ample opportunity to participate in the establishment of his own performance objectives. Thus, the whole concept is oriented to a value system based upon the results achieved; and the results must be concrete and measurable.

When properly administered, Management by Objectives has much to recommend it:

1. It involves the whole organization in the common purpose.

2. It forces top management to think through its purposes, to review them constantly, to relate the responsibilities of individual units to pre-set goals, and to determine their relative importance.

3. It sets practical work tasks for each individual, holds him accountable for their attainment, and demonstrates clearly how his performance fits into the overall effort.

4. It provides a means of assuring that organization goals are eventually translated into specific work tasks for the individual employee.

It is, therefore, virtually impossible to conceive of an effective accountability program that does not operate within the umbrella of the goal-setting process. When properly designed and implemented, goal setting becomes an ideal basis for other forms of performance evaluation. It insures that subordinate goals and role performances are in support of the goals of the higher levels of the organization and that ultimately the institutional purposes will be achieved.

One way of implementing the goal-setting process that has been found useful in education is through the development of a charter of accountability. This approach was originally developed by the Ground Systems Group of the Hughes Aircraft Company. The charter is agreed to by two individuals or groups—one in a superordinate and the other in a subordinate capacity—after consultation, discussion, and negotiation. Ultimately, the entire organization is covered by the series of charters beginning at the top with a major organization unit, say, the English department in a local high school. Each teacher's goals are shaped by his unit's charter of accountability. Each unit head is held accountable for the results specified in his charter, which he draws up and which he and his superiors sign. Ultimately, all charters are combined into a system-wide charter that provides the basis of accountability for the board of education and the superintendent of schools.

A charter contains a statement of purposes, goals, and objectives. *Purpose* constitutes the organization's reason for existence and gives meaning and direction to all its activities. Purposes, therefore, are usually stated in broad inspirational terms.

Goals and *objectives* are the tangible expressions of the organization's purposes. Goals are long-range, concrete, end results specified in measurable terms. Objectives are short-range, specific targets to be reached in a period of one year, also specified in measurable terms.

Specifically, a charter of accountability contains the features on the following list:

1. A statement of system-wide purposes or areas of concern and the purposes of the next level above the unit completing the charter of accountability.
2. A statement of the specific purposes of the unit completing the charter.
3. A description of the functional, administrative, and financial accountability necessary to accomplish the unit's purposes.
4. A set of basic assumptions about the future economic, sociopolitical, professional, and technological developments likely to affect the attainment of goals but which are beyond the control of the accountability unit.
5. A listing of the major goals of the unit to be aimed at for the immediate five-year period.
6. A subseries of performance tasks that provide unit supervisors with definitive targets toward which to orient their specialized efforts and with which to define the resources necessary to accomplish them.
7. Statements of the authority and responsibility necessary to complete these tasks.

Space does not permit the full exposition of the process of establishing a charter of accountability. Very broadly, and quite superficially, it would follow this pattern:

1. A central committee or council composed of representatives of key members of the system—school board, local school boards, union, teachers, parent and community groups—would convene to define the broad purposes of the school system. Putting it simply, their job would be to answer these questions: "What is the business of the school system?" "What are we trying to accomplish?" While the answers to these questions may seem obvious, in practice they are difficult to articulate. Answering them serves the larger purpose of clarifying thinking about the realistic aims of a school system. In business, the definition of purpose has led to dramatic changes in organization structure, business policies, product mix, and, ultimately, in return on investment.

The purposes delineated by this council are then discussed widely in the community. In particular, they serve to determine the major areas of concern of the school system that have been assigned to it by the community. Both the purposes and the areas of concern, however, must be considered at this point to be tentative and subject to modification by lower levels of the system. They will provide, however, the necessary guidelines for the goal-setting process and the development of charters of accountability by the school districts and other lower level units.

2. Each major subunit—school district, division, or department—meets to define its goals and objectives and to prepare its charter of accountability. Since these goals and objectives can differ substantially according to the needs of specific localities, the criteria of accountability will also differ. This is the important, even crucial point that constitutes the major advantage of the goal-setting process. It provides for multiplicity of measures of accountability that are tailored to the needs and hence the goals of specific operating units. The objectives of a principal of an inner-city school will differ from those of a principal of a surburban school, and so must the measures of accountability. Reading grade equivalents may be an appropriate measure of teacher effectiveness in one school and not in the other.

3. The charters of all units are collated and reviewed by the central council or school board with the advice and assistance of the planning and budgeting unit of the office of the superintendent of schools. Appropriate approvals are granted in accordance with existing policy and legislation. Thus, the combined charters constitute *the* charter of accountability for the board of education and the entire school system. While there will be some uniformity to this charter, it is apparent that it will resemble more a patchwork quilt than a seamless cloak and will, therefore, adhere more closely to the reality it attempts to reflect.

4. As each charter is approved, subcharters are developed in the same way for individual units in each district. Obviously, the heads of these units will have had a voice in the formulation of the district charter so that this will not be a new task for them. But in developing the subunit charters in the schools themselves, all the members of the system will ultimately have a voice.

5. Once the charters have been adopted, they are implemented. In some cases, new inputs will eliminate or change previously stated objectives. In others, objectives will be found to be quite unrealistic. Provisions must be made, therefore, to amend the charters of accountability as experience dictates. In most cases, however, it is advisable to stick with the original charter until the year-end review and appraisal of results.

6. The evaluation of the achievement of the period's objectives is made as plans for the next charter are formulated. This is the essence of accountability: results compared to objectives. It is important to note, however, that this evaluation is made not in a punitive, policing climate to check up on people, but rather in a supportive, constructive atmosphere to find out how objectives were achieved and, if they were not, why not. Both parties to this process assume the responsibility for the results and approach the task with the idea of exploring what happened for purposes of problem solving and resetting goals and objectives.

Intervention in the Middle

The implementation of an accountability program depends, to a large extent, on the attitudes and the skills of the supervisory force. If it is skeptical, anxious, or hostile to the plan, it will fail no matter how well it is conceived. This has been the bitter experience of many firms that have attempted to install goal-setting and performance-evaluation programs without first preparing their managers and supervisors to implement them.

Thus, a second essential step in introducing accountability into a school system is the establishment of a massive supervisory development program. Such a program must be practical, intensive, and primarily participative in nature. Its purpose is not merely to disseminate information but rather to change attitudes and to impart specific skills, particularly the skill of conducting accountability interviews with subordinates.

This will not be easy. Most supervisors, principals, and teachers have had no experience with such a program to prepare them for the tasks involved. A development program must be tailor-made to meet their needs.

The development program must also begin at the top with the superintendent and the assistant superintendents. There is a practical reason for this. When presenting this subject matter to middle managers in other organizations, an almost universal response from them is, "Why can't our bosses take this course? They need it more than we do." Since the program content is likely to be quite strange, even revolutionary, to many of the lower middle-management participants, its credibility can be insured only by its being accepted at the highest levels and applied there first.

The program must enable the top-level people to examine the basic assumptions on which they operate and give them as much time as possible to get these assumptions out in the open. The specific objectives of the program would be:

1. To emphasize the influence process in handling subordinates, managers, and supervisors, as well as teachers, and to de-emphasize the formal authority-power-coercion approach to supervision and administration.
2. To provide a deeper understanding of the communications process itself. Such a program must heighten the awareness of the supervisor as to how he comes across best to others and develop his flexibility in dealing with the broad spectrum of personalities encountered in the fulfillment of his responsibilities. Each supervisor should be given an opportunity to prepare a plan for his self-growth and development.
3. To consider ways of dealing with the more routine aspects of teaching by considering job enrichment techniques.
4. To emphasize the socio-psychological realities that education faces today. The program should make supervisors aware that they simply cannot rely on authoritarianism alone to get results with people.

The format of the program should be primarily participative in nature, that is, it should consist of learning experiences and exercises which require the supervisors to participate actively in the training sessions. Frequent use should be made of audiovisual displays, role playing, conference discussions, and case study techniques. Theoretical ideas and concepts that help develop new ways of thinking and approaching problems can be introduced and amplified through specifically designed case studies. The solutions which result from the systematic examination of these case studies should be applied directly to specific school system problems. And, finally, attention must be given to problem areas that may be unique to an individual supervisor.

Intervention at the Base

The third phase of the accountability system, and the most pertinent, is the development of specific instruments and techniques to evaluate how individual members of the school system are performing their assigned roles. Since this phase touches the teachers directly, it is the most difficult and also the most delicate. If it is handled properly, it can accelerate the educational development of the community's children. If it is handled poorly, or indifferently, or as just another routine task (as it so often has been in other public agencies), problems of academic retardation will persist.

Description and discussion of the design, development, and installation of individual performance standards and measures for teachers is beyond the scope of this paper. There are a number of approaches to this effort utilizing both objective and subjective measures. But regardless of the measures and procedures employed, there are some general principles that warrant mention here.

First, an individual teacher accountability program can function effectively only within the context of a goal-setting program, such as the charter of accountability previously described, and a program of continuous supervisory development in coaching and evaluation interviewing.

Second, it must be quite clear from the outset that the prupose of the accountability program is improvement of present role performance. If the measurements and standards developed are used for other purposes, such as discipline, promotion, and salary increases, the program will fail, positively and absolutely. Of course there must be a relationship between the measures of accountability and these other personnel actions, but the relationship must be indirect and antecedent rather than direct and causal.

Third, the immediate intentions of the instruments developed as part of the accountability program should be to provide the teacher (or other professional worker) with feedback on his efforts and to provide him and his supervisor with material for discussions of ways to strengthen his professional performance.

The instruments or standards of measurement of performance must be designed to fulfill two purposes:

1. They must be meaningful and acceptable to the person who is evaluated by them.
2. They must permit quantitative consolidation in the form of means, standard scores, and percentiles to serve as criteria with which to evaluate the department, school, and district achievement of objectives.

Such instruments can be of two basic types:

1. *Results-oriented data.* These are hard data geared to the effects of the teacher's performance—attendance, standardized achievement test scores, grade point averages, etc.
2. *Person-oriented data.* These consist of ratings completed by peers, superiors, and subordinates describing the *style* of the teacher's permance, that is, his initiative, technical competence, interpersonal competence, etc. It is possible to design the instrument so that the person completing it cannot consciously control the outcome.

None of the information obtained at this level should go beyond the school principal except in a consolidated and hence anonymous form.

To insure the acceptance of these instruments, it is necessary that the teachers themselves and their supervisors actively participate in this research, design, and implementation. This is done in two ways. First, in the initial development of the program, teachers and supervisors should actively assist the professional researchers at every stage. Second, and even more important, in the accountability interview, the teacher takes an active role in what is essentially a problem-solving process.

The entire program described in this paper pivots around the accountability interview between supervisor and teacher. If it is conducted well throughout the school system, then the educational process in that community will thrive. If it is done poorly, the whole accountability program will fail and the school system will be in trouble. Therefore, this encounter is crucial.

To make the interview effective, a number of conditions must exist before, during, and after. First, the supervisor must have discussed his own performance with his superior—the principal or the superintendent. He must also have participated in the development of his charter of accountability and that of his school or district. Both the teacher and the supervisor must be familiar with these documents.

They must also be aware of the department's and the school's goals and objectives. The supervisor must have adequate preparation in coaching and interviewing skills. Both the supervisor and the teacher must have met earlier to agree on the dimensions of the teacher's role and on acceptable standards of performance. The teacher must be given adequate time for self-evaluation, and both must have reviewed the data resulting from the accountability instruments referred to above.

During the interview, both discuss the material collected on the teacher's performance. They analyze the teacher's strengths and explore ways of capitalizing on them. They identify areas for improvement, develop an improvement plan, and choose the resources to implement it. The teacher also discusses his professional problems with his supervisor and ways in which the latter can be of greater assistance to him. They establish follow-up schedules with milestones to determine progress. And they put all of this—the plan, the schedule, and the milestones—in writing for subsequent review and follow-up.

This accountability program, sincerely pursued at all these levels, is guaranteed to achieve positive results. There will remain, however, one major obstacle—time. It is obvious that the program will make major demands on a supervisor's time. Consequently, most supervisors will assert that they do not have the time for such a meticulous and detailed approach. In part they will be wrong, and in part they will be right.

They will be wrong, first, because they are not really using the time they now have to maximum advantage. If they are like most managers, they waste a good deal of time in superfluous activities. Secondly, they will be wrong because they are mistaken in their notions of the proper functions of their job. They tend to overemphasize the professional and functional aspects of their responsibilities and to underemphasize the managerial and supervisory concerns that are of paramount importance in the organizational system.

But they will be right because their present school system, like nearly every other organizational system in the United States, requires them to perform many functions that interfere with their basic duties of manager and supervisor.

The answer to this problem, which is one of the chief stumbling blocks to the implementation of an accountability program, seems to lie in a searching examination of the functions performed at each level of supervision. Many of these, upon closer examination, will be found to be delegatable, thus enriching the jobs of their subordinates and freeing them for their real responsibilities of managing one of the most vital enterprises in society—the school system.

Performance Contracting

In recent years, advocates of school reform have championed many causes and proposed many innovative programs, including compensatory education, equitable financing, desegregation, community control, alternative schools, and accountability. Performance contracting, then, must be viewed in relation to this general trend toward reform, and more specifically, as part of the movement toward accountability.

In the first article in this section, James A. Mecklenburger and John A. Wilson discuss some of the pros and cons of performance contracting and analyze the major trends in its use. They evaluate the success of programs in Cheery Creek, Colorado; Texarkana, Arkansas; Grand Rapids, Michigan; New York City; and Gary, Indiana.

In the next article, Reed Martin and Charles Blaschke examine the legal issues involved in the establishment of a performance contract between a school board and private company. They emphasize the need for schools to retain final authority and control over policy making. Much of their discussion is devoted to explaining the need for a "turnkey" clause in a contract. This defines the terms under which the school would take over the operation of a successful program from the contracting agency.

In the final article, Barney M. Berlin reviews some of the research findings relating to performance contracting, concentrating especially on the 1972 OEO report. From his analysis of the research, Berlin questions the effectiveness of performance contracting. He sees it producing little improvement in students' cognitive learning. However, he believes there may be some overlooked benefits of performance contracting in the affective domain of learning, citing such results as increased school spirit, pride in work among students, and greater parental participation.

Learning C.O.D.:
Can the Schools Buy Success?

James A. Mecklenburger and John A. Wilson

One of the newest, most controversial, and perhaps, least understood phrases in the contemporary lexicon of education is "performance contracting." A performance contract, strictly speaking, is a variety of legal contract. The contractor is rewarded according to his measured performance at a specified task. Evelyn Wood Reading Dynamics, for example, has offered such a contract for years: Triple your reading rate, or your money back. Aircraft corporations frequently sign performance contracts. But performance contracting for instructional programs—*paying according to how much children learn*—is new to public schools. There have been fifty performance contracts in education since they began in 1969; there may be fifty again this year.

Performance contracting has a Pandora's Box quality; applying business-military-government procedures to education unlocks debate over a whole series of educational issues.

"Hucksters in the schools!" is the cry of the American Federation of Teachers (AFT). Many educators concur. In contrast, two polls by the National School Board Association during 1970–71 show two-thirds of its members sympathetic to or favoring performance contracting. "Performance contracting does what [teachers] won't do—it rises or falls on *results*, not on schedules and seniority and protected mediocrity," said one school board member. Some performance contract adovates hail the dawning of new school-government-business cooperation; some critics denounce the beginning of an "educational-industrial complex."

The sharpest controversy emerges from the tense alliance that performance contracts create between school people and industry-government people. For example, such tensions nearly wrecked a project in Gary, Indiana, during its first semester in 1970. Don Kendrick, "center manager" of the project, arrived in Gary with experience as a systems analyst in the Air Force and at Lockheed. He considered schooling comparable to aircraft produc-

Dr. Mecklenburger is Director of Research for the National School Boards Association, Evanston, Ill. Dr. Wilson is Director of the School for Public and Environmental Affairs, Indiana University. This article orginally appeared in *Saturday Review* (September 18, 1971). Copyright 1971 by Saturday Review, Inc. It also appears in J. A. Mecklenburger, J. A. Wilson, and R. W. Hostrop (eds.), *Learning C.O.D.: Can the Schools Buy Success?* (Hamden, Conn.: Linnet Books, 1972).

tion—each was a system producing a product, whether airplanes or learning —and made no secret of the comparison.

"I'm a systems analyst," he told one visitor. "I view things analytically. Keep out of emotions. . . Industry says we want a job done. This is the difference [between industry and schools]. You don't have to love the guy next to you on the assembly line to make the product. He puts in the nuts, you put in the bolts, and the product comes out. Teachers can hate me and still get children to learn." As one Gary teacher remarked, "There's no way a man with that attitude can succeed in a school. No way."

The fault was not Kendrick's but was inherent in the situation. Because business and school allies are people with vastly different experience, ideas, expectations, and jargon, merely talking together is sometimes difficult. People who talk of management, cost-effectiveness, needs assessment, and *product* emphasis rouse hostility in people who talk of the whole child, individual differences, *my* classroom, or the learning *process*. Much of the public debate over performance contracting (and over accountability, which is frequently associated with it) has foundered on this rocky language dilemma.

Performance contracts have taken a number of different forms, and the variety is likely to increase in the future. The first such contract between the schools of the twin cities of Texarkana, on the Arkansas-Texas border, and Dorsett Educational Systems stipulated that Dorsett would be paid a certain amount for each child in grades six to eight whose performance in English and mathematics was raised by at least one grade level. In 1970, under a more daring agreement, the Behavioral Research Laboratories (BRL) of Palo Alto, California, contracted to take over completely the organization and administration of one elementary school in Gary, Indiana, for four years—with payment to be based on student achievement. And the most ambitious program, funded by the Office of Economic Opportunity at $6.5 million, resulted in contracts similar to that in Texarkana being negotiated between the schools in eighteen cities and six different performance contractors, involving more than 27,000 children.

Companies with performance contracts in schools presume that schools ought to be "learning systems." The systems idea is not new; it has been applied with varied sophistication and success to military, engineering, city planning, and other enterprises. The most prominent example is the space effort, and one hears the argument "*If we get men to the moon, why can't we teach kids to read?*" Or, "*If industry had 40 percent rejects in its system, it would revise the system; therefore schools too should revise their system.*" Some apostles suggest that schools, like the Apollo missions, should try to be "zero-defect systems."

The jargon surrounding systems ideas is nearly impenetrable. In effect, a system is a goal-oriented enterprise. It is characterized by formal procedures for defining goals, for identifying the tasks necessary to the achievement of these goals, for organizing to accomplish the tasks, for measuring one's success, and for revising the process as experience (data) dictates.

Applied to schools, the goal or product of a system is usually said to be student learning—measurable, observable student learning.

This demand for observable outcomes, for specificity of goals, coincides with pressures within education (associated with B. F. Skinner's behavioral psychology) to define teaching-learning in terms of "behavioral objectives" —that is, precise and observable student behavior. Some contractors now call these "performance objectives." One product of the behavioral objectives movement has been programed instruction in which a student proceeds step by step through a preordained learning sequence until he achieves an objective, as demonstrated on a test. Because such instruction is inexpensive, individual, and above all produces measurable results, programed instruction is integral to virtually all performance contractors' learning systems.

Since materials provide the instruction, teachers' roles change; adults now coordinate the learning system, making certain that each child has the right materials at the right time. Teachers "teach" only when a child needs assistance. Appropriately, in many projects, teachers are now "learning directors" or "instructional managers" and classrooms have become "learning centers."

Several learning systems employ only a few certified teachers, replacing them with paraprofessionals or "assistant learning directors" who are usually local parents. A few systems have replaced teachers entirely—a fact not lost on teacher unions and associations.

The result of these innovations is often praised as "individualized instruction." Advocates of such learning systems assert that children learn at different rates so that group instruction is neither efficient nor effective. Confusion surrounds the term "individualized," however, because many educators use it synonymously with "personalized" or "humanized"—thinking that "individualized" implies regard for each student as a unique human being, capable of freedom of choice in the learning process. A few learning systems foster a personal touch; others pay little heed; most are highly structured, individualizing only the *rate* of instruction.

Neither the systems approach nor individualized instruction is the unique province of performance contractors, however. Other educational technology companies, university and government research laboratories, publishers, and teachers also have experimented with systems approaches. As a Michigan Education Association position paper summarized the situation, "What the performance contractor sells is not new ideas per se, but the way in which new ideas are put together to produce a result. The primary reason for [his] success lies in the fact that he brings to the school a *well thought-out system* and operates the system free and *unencumbered by the school administration of the district.*" [Emphasis theirs.]

Within each school or school system where contracting has occurred and in the larger state and national programs, performance contracting has created pressure toward systems for learning. And some educators have gotten the message. For example, in Grand Rapids, Michigan, Elmer Vruggink, the assistant superintendent for instruction, says that performance contracts have taught him that "sometimes we scatter our efforts too widely; teachers must become more systematic. It is not so much *the* system, but merely being systematic, that will succeed." (Grand Rapids will have twice the number of contracted projects this year [1971] as it had last year.)

Within a learning center, terminology is pseudomedical: Learning managers "diagnose" what the student needs to learn and then "prescribe" the learning sequence each student will follow.

Testing has been the sticky wicket for learning systems, but particularly for performance contractors, whose payment is usually based upon test scores. Most contracts employ individual student scores on standardized achievement tests as the basis for paying the contractor. A number of the nation's leading testing experts have heaped scorn on this procedure, calling performance contracting a gimmick, highly questionable and invalid.

The culprit is the so-called grade-equivalent score. This score implies that a student is above or below grade level. The assumption is that tests provide precise yardsticks of student progress, and educators have allowed parents and school boards to believe in these scores. But these tests are not precise. As measuring devices for individual learning, they have the accuracy more of a fist than a micrometer. Henry Dyer, former vice president of Educational Testing Service, called grade-equivalent scores "statistical monstrosities." The tests yield scores that can be treated as precise data, but these numbers are actually very imprecise. So many factors can influence these scores that they become virtually meaningless. Maturation, testing conditions, the timing of tests, student attitude, and pure chance can create statistical increases that would fulfill a performance contract without the student's learning anything.

In recent months, some performance contracts have moved in more defensible directions—either using different kinds of tests, or employing more statistically reliable applications of standardized tests (which more adequately measure group performance than individual performance), or setting goals not requiring testing.

Nevertheless, scratch almost any performance contract and a defensive scream emerges over testing. Said one superintendent, "For better or worse or right or wrong, that's the way we do it! We let kids into college based on the SAT, and we let them into graduate school based on the Miller Analogy, and we let them into industry based on all kinds of standardized tests." No doubt, the testing and measurement of performance are the Achilles' heel of performance contracting.

How a student should be motivated to proceed through a learning system— especially a student who habitually performs poorly in school—is a question about which contractors differ. Some assert that learning is its own reward. Some presume a bribe—by any other name—at the right moment helps; they use dolls, radios, Green Stamps, hamburgers, and trinkets as rewards or incentives. Some contractors emphasize praise and motivation. Others presume comfortable surroundings will motivate students, so they create colorful, carpeted, air-conditioned learning centers.

Some contractors have adopted the practice of "contingency management," which assumes that if the classroom environment contains appropriate rewards for desirable behavior, undesirable behavior will disappear. A few contractors take this theory seriously and train their staffs to use varied techniques of positive reinforcement.

The most intricate incentive system we witnessed was in Grand Rapids. It was conducted by Alpha Learning Systems, and teachers reinforced both good behavior and good academic work by distributing tokens (rubber washers in elementary school, paper money called "skins" in junior high). For a portion of the school day, youngsters go to a Reinforcing Events Room where they use tokens to pruchase goods and activities they enjoy—for example, jump ropes, puzzles, soft drinks, candy, and toys for elementary children; pinball, billiards, soft drinks, candy, and dance music for adolescents. John Cline, the program director for Alpha, justifies the system in this way:

> When you put kids who are two or three years behind into that social studies class down the hall, and this kid is fifteen years old and reading at a third-grade level, and you say to him, "Read pages fourteen to twenty-one and answer the twelve questions at the end," what you're doing to that kid is saying, "Hey, loser! We want to reassert that you are a dummy! A loser! You have no inherent value!"
>
> And we do this to him time after time, day after day, year after year. Sure the kid believes he's a loser! He doesn't like himself. He doesn't like school. He doesn't like anything.
>
> And to expect that the kid is going to be intrinsically motivated to do anything in school is stupid! The way we justify extrinsic motivation is to say, "We've got to get him motivated. And since it is stupid to assume that he has any inner motivation, let's give him some outward motivation to get him started."
>
> We hear from people that the kid should *want* to succeed. Well, goddamn yeah, he should. But he doesn't.

In the Alpha program, the teachers we met favored contingency management. We were impressed also and agree with Melvin Leasure, president of the Michigan Education Association, who says: "At first it was very hard to accept the extrinsic motivation. When we were able to see how it was used in Grand Rapids, however, we saw that the kids were motivated and that after a while the extrinsic motivation became less and less important. Apparently, it was doing the job without any possibility of permanent damage."

Implicit in the learning systems we have discussed is a mechanical conception of learning: Learning (of certain kinds) can be divided into discrete units; units can be labeled (with objectives) and tested. Students must acquire learnings—as many as possible. The system succeeds when the child tests 100 percent. Learnings are things; since contractors are paid for student learning, learning, by implication, is a commodity to be bought and sold. Most performance contracting so far has tied simple, perhaps ill-conceived, goals to crudely designed monetary rewards for the successful contractor. Perhaps most performance contracts exemplify what Ivan Illich characterized as the school mentality: "Knowledge can be defined as a commodity" since "it is viewed as the result of institutional enterprise [and] the fulfillment of institutional objectives."

However, not all performance contracts have displayed this mentality; and they need not do so. "Performance" can be far more widely construed than it has been. Teaching methods can differ entirely from today's practices. And the use of incentives can be applied to others than private corporations.

We are encouraged by an extraordinary performance-contracted project in Cherry Creek, Colorado, in which teachers, not a corporation, contracted with the school district to try a new idea. "I-team" was a dedicated effort to create within the public school a very personalized program to provide potential dropouts with a meaningful, responsive educational program tailored to them—virtually a "free school" within the public schools. The contract called for a salary bonus to the teachers if the program succeeds in achieving its original objectives. There were ten objectives ranging from changes in attendance patterns to change in academic work, from changes in attitude to change in social behavior.

Outside evaluators, using several different tests, unobtrusive measures, and personal observation, ruled on the program's success (and expressed their own amazement at how successful I-team had been). In the judgment of the evaluators, the performance contract provided a useful incentive for excellent teachers to perform at their best.

Performance contracts, then, need not necessarily purchase rigid learning systems for teaching reading or mathematics. They are one device for making changes in schools, and many kinds of programs could develop under them. John Loughlin, Indiana's state Superintendent of Public Instruction, asserted recently that "the principles inherent in performance contracting are applicable to teachers, universities, and schools. Performance contracts are a process, not a solution within themselves. They take the untried ways out of the ivory tower and put them into the classroom. I see no reason why performance-contracted projects cannot be developed on the campus, in the halls of the state Teachers Association, the National Education Association, or the American Federation of Teachers."

Change is the keynote in talk of performance contracting, and with some justification. In at least some cases, parents see clear proof that kids learn; school boards find a new way to share responsibility and to seek federal funds; superintendents gain prestige as innovators; testing experts acquire some long-awaited attention; work and salary patterns for teachers begin to change; new professions in education begin to emerge; an opening has been made for entrepreneurs; and whole school systems seriously address fundamental educational issues.

There are modest changes, such as better ways to teach reading, to squeeze the tax dollar, or to sell more textbooks; and major changes, such as paying children to learn, ending the autonomy of the classroom teacher, shifting power away from old vested interests, even redefining what school is and what learning is.

It is also claimed that performance contracting stimulates change in the schools generally through the innovative example it gives, through the possibility it provides for school boards to experiment without high risk—they can claim credit for successes and blame the contractor for failures—through the provision of system design and management skills not usually available to the schools, and through simply shaking up the system so that it is easier to get change started and keep it going.

The most elaborate and most formal answer to the question of how performance contracting changes schools has been advanced by Charles Blaschke and Leon Lessinger. Blaschke, drawing upon defense industry procurement procedures, planned the Texarkana project. Lessinger, then an Associate U.S. Commissioner of Education, funded it. Lessinger now invokes Texarkana as the best example of what he calls "educational engineering." This formal and complex process systematically links planning, teaching, and evaluation. Planning is in two parts. All interested parties are consulted until an entire educational project is outlined, based on specified needs—a process called "needs assessments." Then a Request For Proposals (RFP) is issued to competing companies, asking them to bid on the project.

After a contract is agreed upon, an outside evaluator to do the testing and final report and an "educational auditor" to superintend and attest to everyone's honesty (similar to a certified public accountant) are hired. Presumably, everything is the focus of community attention, open, and scrupulously honest. At the end of the year, a project will have had every opportunity to prove itself.

Blaschke has adapted the term "turnkey" from the building trades, where a contractor may accept full responsibility for construction of a building, then turn the keys over to the new owner. Similarly, an educational contractor may run a project for a year or more, then turn it over to the school system. This has occurred in some cities, including Texarkana, where in the third year, beginning this fall [1972], the school system will run the program begun by the contractor.

Some contracts have followed the Lessinger-Blaschke model, from needs assessment to turnkey; but in many contracts, such as the one set up in Gary, the contractor was selected without competitive bidding. Most companies prefer to negotiate performance contracts without competitive bidding. Some contracts dispense with the evaluator, with the school board assuming responsibility for evaluation. Some contracts dispense with the auditor. Similarly, at the end of a project the school may accept the entire program, adopt part of it, or drop the whole thing.

Some experts assert that turnkey is a device for avoiding legal problems. If the contract specifies the school board's intention to turnkey a project, then, it is claimed, it abdicates no responsibility to the contractor. But the question of control of the schools remains one of the most difficult of all those raised by performance contracting.

The Gary contract, calling for the turning over of an entire elementary school, Banneker School, to BRL, was the boldest challenge to date, not only to tradition but also to the education establishment. George Stern, then president of BRL, rejoiced that through the contract BRL had "gained the clout to implement all our ideas." But the reality wasn't as simple as merely signing a contract. Nowhere has the power struggle inherent in performance contracts been more explosive.

In the first skirmish, a summer ago, Indiana Attorney General Theodore Sendak, at the request of the state Department of Public Instruction, expressed his informal opinion that contracting for the operation of a public school by a private corporation would be illegal. School City of Gary (which is the name given to the city's public schools) and BRL felt compelled to modify their contract to reduce somewhat the school board's delegation of authority to the company. In late summer, state Superintendent of Public Instruction Richard D. Wells asked School City to consider planning for one year before beginning the project or, failing that, to hire BRL as consultant only; he offered Gary $20,000 to pay for BRL's consultant services. Not to be co-opted, School City chose to continue in its own direction.

When it became clear that neither Sendak's opinion nor Wells's advice had deterred the contract, the Gary Teacher's Union voted to strike over involuntary teacher transfers and other contract violations. School City countered by seeking a judicial restraining order, after which the union felt constrained to use its own grievance procedures. The results are still being argued.

After extensive investigation, the state Department of Public Instruction in January challenged the legality and quality of the project: Classes were too large; state-adopted textbooks were being ignored; some staff were uncertified; only reading and mathematics had been taught. Some community elements in Gary and some school administrators joined with the state in insisting that subjects other than reading and mathematics be taught. BRL is paid only for reading and math test score gains, although the company contracted to operate the entire school; BRL argued that it had planned from the beginning to phase in a broader curriculum. It was phased in quickly.

"There is nothing uniquely innovative about the Banneker program," asserted a state investigatory report in February, "except the abdication of professional responsibility on the part of School City of Gary and the placement of primary emphasis upon building and maintaining a systems model instead of upon the children and their needs and interests." The State Board of Education decommissioned Banneker School in February, a move which threatened to cost Gary $200,000 in state aid and resulted in adverse national publicity.

Some changes in the program resulted quickly; a change also occurred in the political climate—Governor Edgar D. Whitcomb visited Banneker School just before the March state Board of Education meeting, calling the school a "worthy experiment." The board recommissioned Banneker School.

Finally, under School City's prodding BRL consented to run a 1971 summer program, using Banneker's teachers under BRL guidance, to produce an expanded curriculum that would be suitable for the wide range of academic ability found among the children in the school. Perhaps coincidentally, several BRL and Gary administrators connected with the project will not return this second year.

Similarly, performance contracting upset the national power structure in education. After a series of blistering resolutions at their August convention, the AFT established "listening posts" East, Central, and West to monitor performance contracting; its publications were filled with accusations, many of them embarrassingly accurate. And its *Non-coloring Book on Performance Contracting* is a vicious piece of political cartooning that has been reprinted widely.

The National Education Association (NEA) seemed to want, at first, to respond in the same manner as the AFT, but two of its locals signed contracts with the Office of Economic Opportunity (OEO), forcing the national organization to bite its tongue. The NEA was hardly solid on the issue, in any case. Its Michigan affiliate wrote and spoke very highly of the benefits caused by performance contracts in Michigan, and NEA locals elsewhere were at least respectful of projects in their jurisdiction.

Clearly, the final verdict on performance contracting is far from in. Some contracts have shattered complacency, inspired creativity, improved learning, and turned the spotlight of public attention on the quality of classroom instruction. But others have inspired greed and chicanery, created poor environments for children, and fomented unhealthy dissension.

Performance contracting has as its kernel a powerful idea: Someone other than children must bear the responsibility for whether children learn successfully. Who bears that responsibility, and to what measure, are questions loaded with dynamite. Surround these questions with money, risk, publicity, new teaching strategies, new people, new rhetoric, systems analysis, contingency management, and more, and it is no wonder that this recent, and thus far minuscule, phenomenon has raised such a ruckus in public education.

To date, most performance contracts have been primitive in design, method, and evaluation, their high-flown rhetoric notwithstanding. Results are beginning to be reported. Some projects undoubtedly will appear to do very well; others will be instructive as failures. All should be regarded with the kind of hopeful skepticism that greets the first trial of any new invention.

However, there are signs of emerging sophistication. Here and there, creative and knowledgeable people are questioning the narrow definitions of performance that have bred mostly mechanical teaching of basic skills; they are questioning the evaluation that places wholesale reliance on inappropriate tests; and they are sharpening their contracting skills so that projects of more than publicity value emerge.

If this sophistication grows and triumphs over the hucksters and panacea hounds who also flock to inventions, the performance contracts of the early 1970s could well be the first ripple of a new wave in education.

Contracting for Educational Reform

Reed Martin and Charles Blaschke

Educators have had a year of debate on the Texarkana performance contract experiment, and, with allegations of teaching to the test at the end of that experiment, testing and measurement specialists are now having their day. But beneath all the controversy, a change is taking place, with legal ramifications which will long outlive the educational innovation being considered. The application of contractual principles to educational performance is going to pervade every relationship schools now have. Schools were excited by the idea that under performance contracting they could purchase new packages of instruction; what they are now discovering is that they are contracting for educational reform.

The education of our nation's children is a responsibility carefully delegated in constitutions, statutes, and laws. Those who assume that responsibility— whether teachers or parents or private companies—will find legal consequences to all that they do. The most dramatic current attempt to assume responsibility for education is the involvement of private instructional firms which are willing to be paid on the basis of student performance. The relationship established between a public school and a private company takes the form of a so-called performance contract—a legal document. Thus from the very moment a school becomes interested in performance contracting it must consider the many legal questions involved.

The first such question is whether a local school district is *able* to contract with a private organization to perform instructional tasks. Local education agencies, as creations of the state, are given very limited power to contract. Any contract in excess of that power is void even though both parties may agree to it.

Most schools may contract with outside parties to provide certain services, but those generally are services not imposed upon it by constitutional declaration or by state delegation. As Dean Ringel, of Yale Law School, has observed, where the school is under a *duty* to perform a task, then an attempt to contract out for its performance may be void. Although there are as yet no judicial decisions directly on educational performance contracting, cases

Mr. Martin is an attorney who has negotiated many of the performance contracts in the nation and is an officer of Educational Turnkey Systems, Inc., Washington, D.C. Dr. Blaschke has developed more than three dozen performance contracts and is chief executive officer of Education Turnkey Systems, Inc., Washington, D.C. This article originally appeared in *Phi Delta Kappan* (March 1971). Copyright©1971 by Phi Delta Kappa, Inc. Reprinted by permission.

on the general problem indicate that a controlling factor may be that a school cannot contract for an extended period of time to employ private individuals when public employees have been retained to perform a comparable job.[1]

Thus, having a private company take over the full operation of the school, even with a purpose of doing a "better" job than employees already retained on the public payroll, may raise this legal barrier. This has occurred in one city, and the state attorney general has indicated his misgivings. A more limited contract for services which cannot be provided by the school should come closer to meeting legal requirements.

Assuming, then, that there is the authority to contract for the type of services desired by the school, a second legal obstacle may arise: improper delegation of policy-making powers. States delegate certain educational policy-making functions to the local school, and these powers cannot be further delegated to a private group without an abdication of responsibility on the part of the local school. Cases seem to indicate that courts will examine a school's policy-making role even more closely than its authority to contract. It is not clear where a court might draw the line between policy and other roles in regard to the various educational tasks a school might ask a company to perform, but policy roles must be controlled by the school and not delegated to a company.

Three factors might be considered important in determining whether a school is retaining control of policy matters. First is the school's role in developing the program. If the school invites bids on the basis of specifications which are vague and subject to the bidder's own interpretation, then the school may be allowing the bidder to exercise too much authority. If there is not a bidding process, and the school signs a sole-source contract, there are still problems. A company may convince a school to adopt a certain approach which changes school policy, thus assuming too much authority and really nullifying the contractual relationship.

A second area to consider in the question of control is staff expertise. The school must provide a monitoring and management function during the program in order to retain authority and protect policy-making prerogatives. If the staff does not have the requisite expertise, the company will in reality be in control and the school will have abdicated its responsibility. Many schools secure outside management support not only to increase their capability in planning but also to retain control over the program and all its policy ramifications.

A third area indicating policy control is the basic purpose of the contract. Some schools, unfortunately, perceive performance contracting as a way to

---

[1]Dean Ringel, "The Legal Status of Educational Turnkey Programs." (unpublished memorandum).

contract out their problem students, shrugging responsibility for failure off their backs and onto an outside party which is willing to be paid on the basis of student performance. One cannot really blame overburdened schools for finding such a notion so attractive. One can also understand why performance contracting is viewed as a market development and penetration device by new firms and by firms that have had trouble getting their foot in the door of the local schoolhouse. But contracting out as an end in itself may be a delegation of too much authority. If a program were to be conducted for a specified period of time, then evaluated and either abandoned or absorbed by the school, the school would obviously be retaining full authority. However, if a program might be extended indefinitely, always under contract to an outside agency, then effective control of decisions with policy implications might have passed to the contractor.

The state commissioner of education in Texas, which has four performance contracts under way, drew that line clearly in posing a question to the attorney general of the state:

> May a school district enter into performance contracts with private corporations where such a program is primarily proposed for a study in depth of the utilization of the capability of the private sector as one strategy to facilitate desirable educational reforms, as distinguished from any general plan or movement to contract to private corporations the education of regular public school children?[2]

The attorney general's opinion answered the question in the affirmative.[3] One may assume that a school is on safest legal ground when it specifies in the original contract the procedures for taking over the operation of a successfully demonstrated instructional program. This process has come to be called the *turnkey* phase—when the contractor turns the keys over to the school so that the school can run the program thereafter.

This step also has important educational consequences, for the turnkey phase is what will distinguish the performance contracting movement, hopefully, from past educational panaceas. The "crisis" in public education and particularly Johnny's inability to read has long been with us. Suggestions from the private sector, and even demonstration programs which promise dramatic breakthroughs, have been numerous over the last few years. With billion-dollar federal funding, virtually every school district in America has had the opportunity to participate in some experiment. But few approaches, no matter how successfully they were demonstrated, seem to be able to have a continuing impact.

[2]Letter from Commissioner J. W. Edgar to Attorney General Crawford C. Martin, July 28, 1970.
[3]Opinion No. M-666, August 20, 1970.

The reason is that at the end of a program demonstration there are many reasons why the approach may or may not be adopted by the school system: financial, legal, social, political, and even educational reasons. More important, a variety of parties must cooperate if that adoption is to have impact—administrators, teachers, supervisors, school boards, business officers, taxpayers, and even students. Finally, and most important, changes will have to be made in the way people relate to each other and to an overall goal for the adoption to fit into the system. Unless the right questions are considered by the right people, with the correct changes accompanying the answers to those questions, no program will be able to survive. This has been the history of research and demonstration in education over the last few years—highly successful demonstration of programs which have absolutely no traceable impact as they are spread throughout the system. This could be the history of performance contracting if it were not coupled with the turnkey approach.

The idea of turnkey, both legally and educationally, is to demonstrate a program which can be successfully adopted by the school system. Therefore, the first step is to consult decision makers, beginning with teachers, to see what conditions and constraints they would place upon the program. Why pursue the demonstration of an approach which, if successful in educational terms, would not be acceptable to local decision makers for political, social, or economic reasons? Why demonstrate an approach that would require a facility modification the taxpayers would not underwrite or a use of noncertified instructional personnel which the teacher union would not accept?

The second step, after a successful demonstration, is to ascertain what changes need to be made to adopt the approach and maintain its success. Teachers may need to be retrained; administrators may have to develop new staff relationships; students may have to be rescheduled; a new type of diagnostic testing, found to be effective, might have to be employed; measurable performance outcomes, having proven their value as incentives, might have to be developed.

The third step is to make these changes. Thus, performance contracting plus turnkey determines the terms upon which a school system will accept change, demonstrates the effect change can have, and uses that successful demonstration as leverage to have change adopted. One of those changes must certainly be the incorporation of a monitoring system that provides constant feedback on performance and costs. This would be essential during the demonstration phase to indicate whether any success was being demonstrated; and it is essential afterwards so that a newly adopted system can continue to be changed. This is the second major difference in turnkey. Rather than locking a successfully demonstrated program into the system and forgetting it, the turnkey approach continues to evaluate that program as an input leading toward a total goal. Thus turnkey includes the capacity for continual change.

Legal and educational requirements and ramifications appear to merge in the performance contracting-turnkey process. In any one jurisdiction or a specified set of circumstances the case may differ, but a general set of principles may be stated: The test of an adequate contract is the retention of policy control; the test of policy control is the conclusion of the outside relationship and the adoption of successful approaches; and the test of turnkey is the adoption of reforms that must accompany successful adoption of the new approach. *Thus the principal legal consequence of performance contracting is educational reform.*

As stated in an earlier section, staff capabilities become crucial to the fulfillment of legal responsibilities. A turnkey analysis must be performed which shows what, if any, demonstrated approach is worth adopting; the changes which must accompany and facilitate adoption must be indicated; a strategy for accomplishing those changes must be stated; and a continuing monitoring system must be established to feed new information into this dynamic process of self-renewal. Staff must be trained to perform those tasks.

We have been discussing contracts between schools and companies, but an outside agency is not needed for a performance contract. Despite the characterization that opponents of performance contracting have been trying to instill in the public's mind, performance contracts do not require that big business take over the public schools and displace qualified teachers. Performance contracts can be written internally without private business and under the complete control of the existing licensed teachers. Two of the sites in the Office of Economic Opportunity nationwide experiment in performance contracting are Stockton, California, and Mesa, Arizona, where the contracts are between the school board and the teachers' association.

Thus, performance contracting should not be viewed as a way of linking a new outside force onto the existing educational process. It is a way to rearrange the relationships of all the participants in the educational process, new and old.

Participants who will be affected include the community, parents, teachers, teacher colleges, students, funding agencies, and educational firms. The new relationship of one participant, teachers, can indicate the legal rearrangements that are going to follow from performance contracting. School boards will undoubtedly meet teachers at the bargaining table in the next few months with specific performance objectives or accountability clauses to be written into contracts. If teachers are to be held responsible for student performance, they must be delegated the decision-making authority to choose the learning approach they feel is best for each of their students. This flexibility is the "price" which private contractors demand in exchange for accountability, and must therefore be offered to teachers.

Other relationships will be affected. One can imagine the teacher saying to a parent, "I'll be accountable in the classroom by doing certain tasks if you will perform certain tasks at home." Where money passes directly between a parent and supplier of educational services, that will become an element in the contract. With student performance as a goal, students might withhold performance until demands for a curricular change, for example, are met. Funding agencies may make performance a basis of their relationship with schools. Funds could be required to be related to a measurable output and would be cut off if their use did not appear to make a difference. Thus, the dramatic feature of performance contracting—no results, no pay—which schools have enjoyed in their relationship with private companies, will become a very solemn responsibility of schools *vis-à-vis* funding agencies. Testing and evaluation will play a crucial role, and the test manufacturer will be asked to guarantee the validity of his instrument much as firms are now asked to guarantee the effectiveness of the instructional approach.

Thus, the performance contracting-turnkey approach will have a lasting legal implication for the school's relation with others in the educational process. The basic relationship will become one of consumer versus supplier of educational services, with the contract as a primary instrument in this educational revolution leading to consumer sovereignty. The application of contractual law to educational reform may seem to many to be a slow process, but once it begins, it cannot be stopped.

Performance Contracting—
What Can Be Salvaged?

Barney M. Berlin

Reflecting the unrest of the 1960's, schools have been severely criticized for their failure to educate many of their students. A way of holding the schools accountable for the education of students, particularly in reading and writing has been actively sought, especially in urban areas. Barro summarizes current approaches that utilize the concept of accountability, ranging from improved

Dr. Berlin is Associate Professor and Chairman of the Department of Curriculum and Instruction at Loyola University of Chicago.

management methods to alternative educational systems.[1] One of these approaches to accountability is performance contracting.

It seems obvious that some systematic approach to stating objectives and measuring their achievement is necessary if schools are to be held accountable for the achievement of their students. The assumption is that if the objectives are spelled out clearly, the efficiency of teaching and learning will be increased, and the performance of students on standardized tests will improve. Several corporations have already developed instructional materials based on behavioral objectives. These materials are presently being used in various schools employing performance contracting.

Texarkana, Arkansas, was the first school system to sign a performance contract. Although performance contracts have varied somewhat, they usually involve a business firm agreeing to produce specified learnings in a particular group of children. Payment to the firm is dependent on how much learning takes place, as measured by standardized testing instruments. Generally, contracting companies have concentrated on two subject areas—reading and mathematics, since it is generally agreed that the ability to read and perform mathematical operations are the two most important skills. These may also be the only two areas in which some agreement exists among educators as to what should be measured and how to go about measuring it.

Although some educators believe that specific knowledge and skills, except for basic reading and mathematics, are relatively unimportant, schools are faced with the practical problem that the only kinds of cognitive skills that can presently be measured with ease are those on the lowest levels of Bloom's taxonomy.[2] As for the affective domain, educators seem presently unable to define objectives with enough precision to apply them to performance contracting situations.

The most comprehensive set of experiments with performance contracting was commissioned by the Office of Economic Opportunity, which advertised nationally for bids from school districts and corporations.[3] Of the seventy-seven school districts filing formal applications, eighteen were selected for the experiment. Six of the thirty-one corporations that submitted bids were chosen to conduct the experiments. Each of the six firms was assigned schools in three demographically different districts. The setting of the school districts included urban (New York City, Philadelphia, Seattle, and Dallas), middle-

[1]Stephen M. Barro, "An Approach to Developing Accountability Measures for the Public Schools," *Phi Delta Kappan* (December 1970).

[2]Benjamin S. Bloom *et al.*, *A Taxonomy of Educational Objectives: Handbook I, the Cognitive Domain* (New York: David McKay, 1956).

[3]Data on the OEO experiment are taken from *An Experiment in Performance Contracting: Summary of Preliminary Results*. OEO Pamphlet 3400-5 (Springfield, Va.: National Technical Information Service, U.S. Department of Commerce, 1972).

sized urban (Anchorage, Fresno, Grand Rapids, Hammond, Hartford, Jacksonville, Las Vegas, Portland, and Witchita), and rural (Athens, Georgia; McComb, Mississippi; Rockland, Maine; Selmer, Tennessee; and Taft, Texas). In all cases, the schools met the criteria for eligibility under Title I of the ESEA (Elementary and Secondary Education Act).

To prevent contamination of the data to be gathered from this experiment, experimental and control groups were established in different schools in each selected district. The one-hundred students in each grade who scored lowest on school-administered reading and achievement tests were assigned to the experimental and control groups for the study. The fifty students scoring next lowest on the tests served as an in-school check and potential replacement pool for any of the originally selected students who might be unable to participate.

The firms chosen for the experiment were allowed considerable freedom in structuring the learning environment. They were able to use materials they chose and to restructure the classroom organization and personnel. Utilization of paraprofessionals ranged from a low of 32 percent of the total staff in one project, to 100 percent in another. Adult/student ratios varied from 1–5 to as high as 1–20, with the median around 1–13 (two adults, one class of children). Some of the firms relied heavily on incentives or frequently awarded prizes to students.

As for teaching methods, five of the six firms relied heavily on the classroom teacher but used instructional tapes and cassettes as supplementary or reinforcement material. Contamination of data and teaching for the test had to be avoided, if at all possible, and an appropriate evaluation instrument had to be selected. Steps were taken to insure that the companies did not find out which test was to be administered. Payment to the contractors was based on interim testing as well as the final evaluation.

Analysis of the data obtained from pre- and post-testing at all sites revealed no significant differences between control and experimental groups in grades 1 through 3 and 7 through 9 in reading or math after one year.

The differences between the control and experimental groups are negligible and even favor the control groups at times (see Table 1). The OEO report concluded: "These overall differences are so slight that we can conclude that performance contracting was no more effective in (teaching) either reading or math than the traditional classroom methods of instruction."

To avoid the possibility that combining all the data masked differences between sites or among different groups of children, further analysis was undertaken. In one set of analyses, students at the 20th, 40th, 50th, 60th, and 80th percentiles were compared. Although students at the 80th percentile made greater gains during one year than students at the 20th percentile, the differences between the experimental and control groups were negligible in both reading and mathematics.

TABLE 1

Mean Gains of Experimental and Control Students Across All Sites*

READING			MATHEMATICS	
	Experimental Gain[†]	Control Gain	Experimental Gain	Control Gain
GRADE 1	NA**	NA	NA	NA
GRADE 2	.4	.5	.5	.5
3	.3	.2	.4	.4
7	.4	.3	.6	.6
8	.9	1.0	.8	1.0
9	.8	.8	.8	.8

*OEO Report 3400–5, p. 18.
†Because readiness tests, rather than achievement tests were used as pre-tests, no base line exists.
**Gains: in years.

The possibility that certain sites produced significant results that were masked by combining the data for all sites was also investigated. Testing conditions were not uniform and were unsatisfactory at some sites. Despite difficulties in the test situation, no pattern of site superiority emerged from the data, although at some grade levels at single sites, the experimental group did appear to perform slightly better than the control group. Possibly these differences were caused by the experimental methods, but since no consistent pattern or significant difference between control and experimental group means emerged, there is no reason to assume that one method or company proved superior overall to the usual classroom procedures. As the OEO report concludes:

> Thus, despite all the uncertainties that inevitably surround any-
> thing involving the testing of human beings, the results from the
> performance contracting experiment point with remarkable con-
> sistency to the conclusion that there were no significant differences
> in the achievement gains of the experimental and control groups.
> Not only did both groups do equally poorly in terms of overall
> averages, but also these averages were very nearly the same in
> each grade, in each subject, for the best and worst students in the
> sample, and, with few exceptions, in each site. Indeed, the most
> interesting aspect of these conclusions is their very consistency.
> This evidence does not indicate that performance contracting will
> bring about any great improvement in the educational status of
> disadvantaged children.

By now, some readers may have decided that the OEO findings are conclusive. Not necessarily so. Basing his criticisms on an analysis of the report prepared by the Battelle Memorial Institute[4] (the testing and analysis contractor for the OEO) Saretsky contends, "What the OEO actually did was compare atypical (above average) performance of its control groups to the performance of its experimental (performance contracting) groups."[5] He attributes the lack of differences between the experimental and control groups to three factors:

1. The John Henry effect (sometimes called the Avis effect). The teachers of the control groups try harder to avoid being shown up, producing higher than normal results.
2. There is a possibility that the control and experimental groups were not equivalent in terms of aptitude and prior educational achievement. One or more control groups may have had higher mean scores than the corresponding experimental group at the mean outset.
3. The experimental conditions did not provide for control of the traditional curricula (all control classes were assumed to be "traditional") before or during the experimental period. In other words, although stringent conditions were imposed on the experimental group, the control group was not really monitored. Thus, the curriculum in the control group is not precisely known.

In comparing Saretsky's paper with the OEO report, we find that the interpretation and emphasis given the data depended on the point of view of the authors. Both documents, for example, reported a gain of ten months for both control and experimental groups at the 9th grade in the area of mathematics. Saretsky, however, pointed out that in the preceding school years, the prorated gain in 9th grade math was six or seven months, thus possibly supporting his contention that the John Henry effect was operating. The OEO, on the other hand, merely pointed out that the experimental and control groups had achieved at the same level.

As another example, Saretsky stated that the Battelle report indicated "above average control group gains (greater than expected, up to 1.6 years) in a majority of the eighteen experimental sites during the experiment." The OEO report stated "While there were a few apparent successes or failures among the sites, in 80 percent of the cases, there was no evidence of significant differences in the gains of the experimental and control groups."[6] Both statements can be derived from the same set of data.

Another question that arises is whether the standardized achievement tests (or any standardized achievement test) used in the OEO experiment produce

[4]Battelle Memorial Institute, *Interim Report on the OEO Experiment in Performance Contracting* (Springfield, Va.: National Technical Information Service, U.S. Department of Commerce, 1972).

[5]Gary Saretsky, "The OEO P.C. Experiment and the John Henry Effect," *Phi Delta Kappan* (May 1972).

[6]OEO Pamphlet 3400-5, *op. cit.*, p. 22.

valid measures of student gain or loss. Stake investigated numerous measurement devices used in performance contracts, analyzed their faults, and cautioned that all results should be examined carefully.[7]

Some of the performance contract companies have been suspected of teaching to the test. It does appear that some performance contractors may have spent an inordinate amount of class time on reading and math, thus partially accounting for some of the gains. Because of predetermined ideologies, business commitments, and monetary considerations, it may be that some companies and even "independent" evaluators manipulated statistics in favor of the experimental groups.

Thus we are at a standstill. Some people think performance contracting is a workable concept, and others are convinced that it is just another transient educational fad. Farr and his associates conducted an experiment that seems to show that it is possible to produce gains on tests without teaching content (sort of the ultimate in performance contracting).[8] Farr and his colleagues developed a mythical performance contract and tested a group of students on a standardized reading test (Nelson Teading Test, 1962). Four weeks later the students were retested without any intervening reading instruction. A control group was also tested and retested. The scales of the experimental group were compared with those of the control group. Since both groups had been tested and retested, the practice effect was accounted for in the data. The only difference in the testing was that the experimental group was given special instructions. Students were told to try to improve their score on the previous test and were offered various prizes—ranging from candy bars to radios—if they improved by even one point.

Naturally, human nature was victorious. Enough students in the experimental group scored higher than the mean gain of the control group to enable the "contractor" to earn a mythical net profit of $3,000 on his investment of $75 in prizes. Because the use of rewards is common in many performance contracts, the results of this experiment should lead to caution in evaluating the results of these programs.

At this point, it seems appropriate to mention three aspects of performance contracting that merit further consideration:

1. *Are we choosing the wrong experimental group?* Perhaps the lack of success of the performance contracting programs can be attributed to the decision to work with the most educationally disadvantaged students. The concept may prove more successful with students of average ability, or even educationally advantaged students, who are at grade

[7]Robert E. Stake, "Testing Hazards in Performance Contracting," *Phi Delata Kappan* (June 1971).

[8]Roger J. Farr, Jr., Jaap Tuinman, and B. Elgit Blanton, "How To Make a Pile in Performance Contracting," *Phi Delta Kappan* (February 1972).

level or above. If performance contracting has failed with disadvantaged students, it is not the first project to fail with this target population.

2. *Are we measuring the gains of performance contracting appropriately?* In addition to the questions of choice of instrument, we also should consider the possibility that higher intellectual processes may be ignored by the evaluative devices. The concentration on individualized study, characteristic of most performance contracting programs, may have aided in the development of such skills as application, analysis, and synthesis, which tests do not measure.

3. *Is there some benefit to the schools even if there are no significant differences in the achievement rates of the experiment and control groups?* The opportunity to reorganize the staff, experiment with new materials, or provide for individual differences may justify a district's development of a performance contract with an outside agency. In addition, the author's observations of the Banneker School in Gary indicate that school spirit, pride in work, and parental participation have increased since the development of the performance contract project. Affective changes, even if produced by the Hawthorne effect, may offer a valid rationale for proceeding with performance contracting.

As with other aspects of education, we really do not know all the answers about performance contracts. The old cliché is still valid: we do not know what works with whom under what conditions.

Limitations of
Accountability Tests
and Measurements

There appear to be several weaknesses and limitations in the testing and measurement procedures employed with accountability plans and programs involving performance contracting. The implications of this fact are bleak. At best, more effective and appropriate test instruments and means for interpreting test scores will have to be devised. At worst, these problems may prove insurmountable and the present enthusiasm for accountability may be entirely misplaced.

In the first article, Ralph W. Tyler contends that the achievement tests now used to measure learning outcomes in accountability programs yield misleading and faulty data. These norm-referenced tests, according to Tyler, only indicate where the student stands in relation to a larger group. They do not include enough questions dealing with material covered by the student during the term or school year to yield an adequate profile of actual learning achieved. Tyler believes that criterion-referenced tests that measure specified learning outcomes should be used with accountability plans. These kinds of tests, however, are only at the beginning stages of development.

Robert E. Stake ends this section with a discussion of the problems involved in testing students for performance contracting. In particular, Stake focuses on the technical errors and misinterpretations possible in testing and evaluating test scores, and on the temptations offered to teach to the test. He also explains why the profession should be apprehensive about appraising the teaching-learning process solely on the basis of standardized tests.

Testing for Accountability

Ralph W. Tyler

The growing concern about accountability has put new emphasis on measuring what and how much a student has learned in a short period of time. To measure educational outcomes in such a period requires tests designed for this purpose; and the problem for administrators is that most tests currently available are not very suitable.

A good example of the problem is in the area of performance contracting, where schools contract for instruction with private companies on a fee arrangement based on student performance. Since it appears that performance contracts will generally be let to cover students considered to be low achievers from disadvantaged environments, the standard achievement tests in common use do not furnish a dependable measure of how much those children have learned during one school year or less.

They were not constructed to do so.

A typical achievement test is explicitly designed to furnish scores that will arrange the pupils on a line from those most proficient in the subject to those least proficient. The final test questions have been selected from a much larger initial number on the basis of tryouts and are the ones which most sharply distinguished pupils in the tryouts who made high scores on the total test from those who made low scores. Test questions were eliminated if most pupils could answer them or if few pupils could answer them, since these did not give much discrimination.

As a result, a large part of the questions retained for the final form of a standard test are those that 40 to 60 percent of the children were able to answer. There are very few questions that represent the things being learned either by the slower learners or the more advanced ones. If a less-advanced student is actually making progress in his learning, the typical standard test furnishes so few questions that represent what he has been learning that it will not afford a dependable measure for him. The same holds true for advanced learners.

Dr. Tyler is former Dean of Education at The University of Chicago and Director Emeritus of the Center for Advanced Study in the Behavioral Sciences of Stanford University. This article originally appeared in *Nation's Schools* (December 1970). © Copyright 1970 by McGraw-Hill, Inc. Reprinted by permission.

This is not a weakness in the test in serving the purpose for which it was designed. The children who made lower scores had generally learned fewer things in this subject than those who made higher scores and could, therefore, be dependably identified as less proficient. Furthermore, a good standard test has been administered to one or more carefully selected samples, usually national, regional, or urban samples, of children in the grade for which the test was designed. The scores obtained from these samples provide norms for the test against which a child's score can be related.

These tests called *norm-referenced tests*, thus provide dependable information about where the child stands in his total test performance in relation to the norm group. But when one seeks to find out whether a student who made a low score has learned certain things during the year, the test does not include enough questions covering the material on which he was working to furnish a dependable answer to that question.

This leads to another problem encountered when one attempts to measure what a child learns in a school year or less. In the primary grades, particularly, each child's learning is dependent on what he had already learned before the year began and what sequence he follows. For example, in reading, some children enter the first grade already able to read simple children's stories and newspaper paragraphs. Measures of what they learn during the first should be based on samples of reading performance that go beyond this entry level.

On the other extreme, some children enter the first grade with a limited oral vocabulary and without having distinguished the shapes of letters or noted differences in their sounds. Measures of what such a child learns during the first year must take off from his entering performance and be based on the learning sequence used in his school to help him acquire the vocabulary and language skills that are involved in the later stages of reading instruction.

A standardized test, however, is designed to be used in schools throughout the nation, despite the different learning sequences they have and with children coming from a variety of backgrounds and at various stages of learning in the field covered by the test. For this reason, it cannot include enough questions appropriate to each child's stage of development to measure reliably what he has learned during a single school year.

Recognizing that norm-referenced tests can provide dependable information on the relative standing of children, but cannot reliably measure what a child has learned or how much he has learned in a year or less, efforts are now under way to construct and utilize tests that are designed to sample specified knowledge, skills and abilities and to report what the child knows and can do of those matters specified. Since the criterion for a performance contract is that each child will learn specified things, a test that samples them is called a *criterion-referenced* test.

For example, in primary reading, the children who enter without having learned to distinguish letters and sounds might be tested by the end of the year on letter recognition, association of letters with sounds, and word-recognition of one hundred most common words. For each of these specified "things to be learned," the child would be presented with a large enough sample of examples to furnish reliable evidence that he could recognize the letters of the alphabet, he could associate the appropriate sounds with each letter, alone and in words, and he could recognize the one hundred most common words. A child has demonstrated mastery of specified knowledge, ability or skill when he performs correctly 85 percent of the time. (Some small allowance, like 15 percent, is needed for lapses common to all people.)

At a higher level of initial performance, a group of children may be expected to read and comprehend typical newspaper paragraphs, simple directions for making or doing something, and so on. Similar specifications are made in arithmetic and in writing. Science and the social studies represent greater problems because of the variations in content and the lack of agreement on essential objectives.

The National Assessment of Educational Progress utilizes criterion-referenced tests and reports to the public about the performance of various categories of children and youth rather than individuals. The public is given the percentage of each group—nine-year-olds, thirteen-year-olds, seventeen-year-olds, and young adults—who know certain facts, can use certain principles in explaining phenomena, are able to do certain things. The reports reveal the exercises that were used and give the percentage of each group who answered the question correctly or who demonstrated the ability or skill involved. The public can get a better grasp of what children and youth are learning by these reports than by trying to interpret abstract scores.

The need for criterion-referenced tests is particularly acute when a contractor undertakes to aid the education of disadvantaged children. Currently used standard tests are not satisfactory tools to appraise the learning of disadvantaged children that can be expected in a single school year. Because most of the disadvantaged begin the year at much earlier stages than a majority of pupils, the standard tests developed for that grade include very few questions that represent what these children are learning.

For this reason, when such a test is given at the beginning of the year and a second test at the end of the year, the changes in score for an individual child may largely be chance variations, since both scores are based on very small samples of knowledge, abilities or skills to these children could respond. Furthermore, since the number of questions on which the initial score is based is small, coaching for these particular items can give a large relative gain. For example, if a child answered four questions correctly in the initial test, being able to answer four more in the final test will place him very much higher on the relative score of a standard test than would a gain of four points when his initial score was 40.

This fact increases the temptation for coaching in the case of contracts involving disadvantaged children. Criterion-referenced tests constructed for the learning sequences actually being followed will include a much larger sample of appropriate questions.

Although there are few criterion-referenced tests presently available, if performance contracting continues to expand rapidly, both schools and contractors will soon recognize that they do not have the tests they need to furnish dependable measures of performance. Publishers may well respond by a crash program of criterion-referenced test development.

Testing Hazards in Performance Contracting

Robert E. Stake

In the first federally sponsored example of performance contracting for the public schools, Dorsett Educational Systems of Norman, Oklahoma, contracted to teach reading, mathematics, and study skills to over 200 poor-performance junior and senior high school students in Texarkana. Commercially available, standardized, general-achievement tests were used to measure performance gains.

Are such tests suitable for measuring specific learnings? To the person little acquainted with educational testing, it appears that performance testing is what educational tests are for. The testing specialist knows better. General achievement tests have been developed to measure correlates of learning, not learning itself.

Such tests are indirect measures of educational gains. They provide correlates of achievement rather than direct evidence of achievement. Correlation of these test scores with general learning is often high, but such scores corre-

Dr. Stake is Professor of Education and Associate Director of the Center for Instructional Research and Curriculum Evaluation at the University of Illinois (Urbana). This article originally appeared in *Phi Delta Kappan* (June 1971). Copyright © 1971 by Phi Delta Kappa, Inc. Reprinted by permission.

late only moderately with performance on many specific educational tasks. Tests can be built to measure specific competence, but there is relatively little demand for them. Many of those tests (often called criterion-referenced tests) do a poor job of predicting later performance of either a specific or a general nature. General achievement tests predict better. The test developer's basis for improving tests has been to work toward better prediction of later performance rather than better measurement of present performance. Assessment of what a student is now capable of doing is not the purpose of most standardized tests. Errors and hazards abound, especially when these general achievement tests are used for performance contracting. Many of the hazards remain even with the use of criterion-referenced tests or any other performance observation procedures.

One of the hazards in performance contracting is that many high-priority educational objectives—for various reasons and in various ways—will be cast aside while massive attention is given to other high-priority objectives. This hazard is not discussed here. This article will identify the major obstacles to gathering direct evidence of performance gain on targeted objectives.

Errors of Testing

Answering a *National School Board Journal* [November 1970] questionnaire on performance contracting, a New Jersey board member said:

> Objectives must be stated in simple, understandable terms. No jargon will do and no subjective goals can be tolerated. Neither can the nonsense about there being some mystique that prohibits objective measurement of the educational endeavor.

Would that our problems withered before stern resolve. But neither wishing nor blustering rids educational testing of its errors.

Just as the population census and the bathroom scales have their errors, educational tests have theirs. The technology and theory of testing are highly sophisticated; the sources of error are well known.[1] Looking into the psychometrist's meaning of a theory of testing, one finds a consideration of ways to analyze and label the inaccuracies in test scores. There is a mystique, but there is also simple fact: no one can eliminate test errors. Unfortunately, some errors are large enough to cause wrong decisions about individual children or school district policy.

Some educators and social critics consider the whole idea of educational testing to be a mistake. Unfortunate social consequences of testing, such as the perpetuation of racial descrimination and pressures to cheat, continue to

[1]Frederick M. Lord and Melvin R. Novick, *Statistical Theories of Mental Test Scores* (Reading, Mass.: Addison-Wesley, 1968).

be discussed. But, as expected, most test specialists believe that the promise in testing outweighs these perils. They refuse responsibility for gross misuse of their instruments and findings and concentrate on reducing the errors in tests and test programs.

Some technical errors in test scores are small and tolerable. But some testing errors are intolerably large. Today's tests can, for example, measure vocabulary word-recognition skills with sufficient accuracy. They cannot, however, adequately measure listening comprehension or the ability to analyze the opposing sides of an argument.

Contemporary test technology is not refined enough to meet all the demands. In performance contracting the first demand is for assessment of performance. Tests do their job well when the performance is highly specific— when, for example, the student is to add two numbers, recognize a misspelled word, or identify the parts of a hydraulic lift. When a teacher wants to measure performances that require more demanding mental processes, such as conceptualizing a writing principle or synthesizing a political argument, performance tests give us less-dependable scores.[2]

Many educators believe that the most human of human gifts—the emotions, the higher thought processes, interpersonal sensitivity, moral sense—are beyond the reach of psychometric testing. Most test specialists disagree. While recognizing an ever-present error component, they believe that anything can be measured. The credo was framed by E. L. Thorndike in 1918: "Whatever exists at all exists in some amount." Testing men believe it still. They are not so naive as to think that any human gift will manifest itself in a 45-minute paper-and-pencil test. They do believe that, given ample opportunity to activitate and observe the examinee, any trait, talent, or learning that manifests itself in behavior can be measured with reasonable accuracy. The total cost of measuring may be one hundred times that of administering the usual tests, but they believe it can be done. The final observations may rely on professional judgment, but this could be reliable and validated judgment. A question for most test specialists, then, is not "Can complex educational outcomes be measured?" but "Can complex educational outcomes be measured with the time and personnel and facilities available?"

When it is most important to know whether or not a child is reading at age-level, we call in a reading specialist, who observes his reading habits. She might test him with word recognition, syntactic decoding, and paragraph-comprehension exercises. She would retest where evidence was inconclusive. She would talk to his teachers and his parents. She would arrive at a clinical description—which might be reducible to a statement such as "Yes, Johnny is reading at or above age-level."

[2]Benjamin S. Bloom et al., A Taxonomy of Educational Objectives: Handbook I, the Cognitive Domain (New York: David McKay, 1956).

The scores we get from group reading tests can be considered estimates of such an expert judgment. These objective test scores correlate positively with the more valid expert judgments. Such estimates are not direct measurements of what teachers or laymen mean by "ability to read," nor are they suitably accurate for diagnostic purposes. Achievement gains for a sizable number of students will be poorly estimated. It is possible that the errors in group testing are so extensive that—when fully known—businessmen and educators will refuse to accept them as bases for contract reinbursement.

Classroom teachers and school principals have tolerated standardized test errors because they have not been obligated to make crucial decisions on the basis of test scores. Actually, in day-to-day practice they seldom use test scores. When they do, they combine them with other knowledge to estimate a child's progress in school and to guide him into an appropriate learning experience. They do not use tests as a basis for assessing the quality of their own teaching.

In performance contracting, the situation is drastically changed; tests are honored as the sole basis for contract reimbursement. The district will pay the contractor for performance improvement. An error in testing means money misspent. Course completion and reimbursement decisions are to be made without reliance on the knowledge and judgment of a professional observer, without asking persons who are closest to the learning (the teacher, the contractor, and the student) whether or not they *see* evidence of learning. Decisions are to be made entirely by objective and independent testing. Numerous human errors and technical misrepresentations will occur.

Which Test Items?

It is often unrealistic to expect a project director to either find or create paper-and-pencil test items, administrable in an hour to large numbers of students by persons untrained in psychometric observation and standardized diagnostics, objectively scorable, valid for purposes of the performance contract, and readily interpretable. The more complex the training, the more unrealistic the expectation. One compromise is to substitute criterion test items measuring simple behaviors for those measuring the complex behaviors targeted by the training. For example, the director may substitute vocabulary-recognition test items for reading-comprehension items or knowledge of components for the actual dismantling of an engine. The substitution may be reasonable, but the criterion test should be validated against performances directly indicated by the objectives. It almost never has been. Without the validation the educator should be skeptical about what it is that the test measures.

It is always unrealistic to expect that the payoff from instruction will be apparent in the performances of learners at test-taking time. Most tests evoke relatively simple behavior. Ebel wrote:

> . . . most achievement tests . . . consist primarily of items testing specific elements of knowledge, facts, ideas, explanations, meanings, processes, procedures, relations, consequences, and so on.[3]

He went on to point out that more than simple recall is involved in answering even the simplest vocabulary item.

Much more complex behavior is needed for answering a reading-comprehension item. These items clearly call for more than the literal meanings of the words read. The student must paraphrase and interpret—what we expect readers to be able to do.

These items and ones for problem solving and the higher mental processes do measure high-priority school goals, but growth in such areas is relatively slow. Most contractors will not risk basing reimbursement on the small chance that evidence of growth will be revealed by *these* criterion tests. Some of the complex objectives of instruction will be underemphasized in the typical performance-contract testing plan.

The success of Texarkana's first performance-contract year is still being debated. Late winter (1969–70) test results looked good, but spring test results were disappointing.[4] Relatively simple performance items had been used. But the "debate" did not get into that. It started when the project's "outside evaluator" ruled that there had been direct coaching on most, if not all, of the criterion test items, which were known by the contractor during the school year. Critics claimed unethical "teaching for the test." The contractor claimed that both teaching and testing had been directed toward the same specific goals, as should be the case in a good performance contract. The issue is not only test choice and ethics; it includes the ultimate purpose of teaching.

Educators recognize an important difference between preparation for testing and direct coaching for a test. To prepare an examinee, the teacher teaches within the designated knowledge-skill domain and has the examinee practice good test-taking behavior (for example, don't spend too much time on overly difficult items; guess when you have an inkling though not full knowledge; organize your answer before writing an essay) so that relevant knowledge-skill is not obscured. Direct coaching teaches the examinees how to make correct responses to specific items on the criterion test.

This is an important difference when test items cover only a small sample of the universe of what has been taught or when test scores are correlates,

[3]Robert L. Ebel, "When Information Becomes Knowledge," *Science* (January 1971).
[4]Dean C. Andrew and Lawrence H. Roberts, "Final Evaluation Report on the Texarkana Dropout Prevention Program," Magnolia, Arkansas: Region VIII Education Service Center, July 20, 1970 (mimeo).

rather than direct measurements, of criterion behavior. It ceases to be important when the test is set up to measure directly and thoroughly that which has been taught. In this case, teaching for the test is exactly what is wanted.

Joselyn pointed out that the performance contractor and the school should agree in advance on the criterion procedure, though not necessarily on the specific items.[5] To be fair to the contractor, the testing needs to be reasonably close to the teaching. To be fair to parents, the testing needs to be representative of the domain of abilities *they* are concerned about. A contract to develop reading skills would not be satisfied adequately by gains on a vocabulary test, according to the expectations of most teachers. All parties need to know how similar the testing will be to the actual teaching.

Unfortunately, as Anderson observed, the test specialist has not developed scales for describing the similarity between teaching and testing.[6] This is a grievous failing. Educators have no good way to indicate how closely the tests match the instruction.

There are many ways for criterion questions to be dissimilar. They can depart from the information taught by: (1) syntactic transformation; (2) semantic transformation; (3) change in content or medium; (4) application, considering the particular instance; (5) inference, generalizing from learned instances; and (6) implication, adding last-taught information to generally known information. For examples of some of these transformations, see Table 1 (page 112).

For many students the appropriateness of these items depends on prior and subsequent learning as well as on the thoroughness of teaching. Which items are appropriate will have to be decided at the scene. The least and most dissimilar items might be quite different in their appropriateness. The reading-comprehension items of any standardized achievement battery are likely to be more dissimilar to the teaching of reading than any of the "dissimilarities" shown in Table 1. Immediate instruction is not properly evaluated by highly dissimilar items, nor is scholarship properly evaluated by highly similar items. Even within the confines of performance contracting, both evaluations are needed.

For the evaluation of instruction, a large number of test items are needed for each objective that in the opinion of the teachers directly measure increase in skill or understanding. Items from standardized tests, if used, would be included item by item. For each objective, the item pool would cover all aspects

[5]E. Gary Joselyn, "Performance Contracting: What It's All About." Paper presented at the Truth and Soul in Teaching Conference of the American Federation of Teachers, Chicago, January, 1971.
[6]Richard C. Anderson, "Comments on Professor Gagné's Paper," in *The Evaluation of Instruction*, M. C. Wittrock and David E. Wiley, eds. (New York: Holt, Rinehart & Winston, 1970), pp. 126–33.

of the objective. A separate sample of items would be drawn for the pretest and posttest for each student, and instructional success would be based on the collective gain of all students.

Creating such a pool of relevant, psychometrically sound test items is a major, but necessary, undertaking. For example, (Dorsett indicated the desirability of such an item pool in the original Texarkana proposal.) It is a partial safeguard against teaching for the test and against the use of inappropriate criteria to evaluate the success of instruction.

What the Scores Mean

At first, performance contracting seemed almost a haven for the misinterpretation of scores. Contracts have ignored (1) the practice effect of pretesting (not discussed here because of space limitations), (2) the origins of grade equivalents, (3) the "learning calendar," (4) the unreliability of gain scores, and (5) regression effects. Achievement may be spurious. Ignoring any one of these five is an invitation to misjudge the worth of the instruction.

Standardized achievement tests have the appealing feature of yielding grade-equivalent scores. Each raw score, usually the number of items right, has been translated into a score indicating (for a student population forming a national reference group) the average grade placement of all students who got this raw score. These new scores are called "grade equivalents." Raw scores are not very meaningful to people unacquainted with the particular test; the grade equivalents are widely accepted by teachers and parents. Grade equivalents are common terminology in performance contracts.

Unfortunately, grade equivalents are available from most publishers only

---

TABLE 1

An Example of Transformations of
Information Taught into Test Questions.

Information taught:	Pt. Barrow is the northernmost town in Alaska.
Minimum transformation question:	What is the northernmost town in Alaska?
Semantic-syntactic transformation question:	What distinction does Pt. Barrow have among Alaskan villages?
Context-medium transformation question:	The dots on the adjacent map represent Alaskan cities and towns. One represents Pt. Barrow. Which one?
Implication questions:	What would be unusual about summer sunsets in Pt. Barrow, Alaska?

for tests, not for test items. Thus the whole test needs to be used, in the way prescribed in its manual, if the grade equivalents are to mean what they are supposed to mean. One problem of using whole tests was discussed in the previous section. Another problem is that the average annual "growth" on most standardized tests is only a few raw-score points. Consider in Table 2 the difference between a grade equivalent of 5.0 and 6.0 within four of the most popular test batteries.

Most teachers do not like to have their year's work summarized by so little change in performance. Schools writing performance contracts perhaps should be reluctant to sign contracts for which the distinction between success and failure is so small. But to do so requires the abandonment of grade equivalents.

For most special instructional programs, criterion tests will be administered at the beginning of and immediately following instruction, often in the first and last weeks of school. A great deal of distraction occurs during those weeks, but other times for pretesting and posttesting have their hazards, too. Recording progress every few weeks during the year is psychometrically preferred, but most teachers are opposed to "all that testing."

Children learn year-round, but the evidence of learning that gets inked on pupil records comes in irregular increments from season to season. Winter is the time of most rapid advancement, summer the least. Summer, in fact, is a period of setback for many youngsters. Beggs and Hieronymus found punctuation scores to spurt more than a year between October and April but to drop almost half a year between May and September.[7] Discussing their reading test, Gates and MacGinitie wrote:

> . . . in most cases, scores will be higher at the end of one grade than at the beginning of the next. That is, there is typically some loss of reading skill during the summer, especially in the lower grades.[8]

The first month or two after students return to school in the fall is the time for getting things organized and restoring scholastic abilities lost during the summer. According to some records, spring instruction competes poorly with other attractions. Thus, the learning year is a lopsided year, a basis sometimes for miscalculation. Consider the results of testing shown in Table 3 (page 114).

The six-week averages in Table 3 are fictitious, but they represent test performance in many classrooms. The mean growth for the year appears to be 1.3 grade equivalents. No acknowledgement is made that standardized test

---

[7]Donald L. Beggs and Albert N. Hieronymus, "Uniformity of Growth in the Basic Skills Throughout the School Year and During the Summer," *Journal of Educational Measurement* (Summer 1968).

[8]Arthur I. Gates and Walter H. MacGinitie, *Technical Manual for the Gates-MacGinitie Reading Tests* (New York: Teachers College Press, Columbia University, 1965), p. 5.

TABLE 2
Gain in Items Right Needed to Advance One Grade Equivalent on Four Typical Achievement Tests.

	Grade equivalent		Needed for an improvement of one grade equivalent
	5.0	6.0	
Comprehensive Test of Basic Skills, Level 3: Reading Comprehension	20	23	3 items
Metropolitan Achievement Test, Intermediate Form B: Spelling	24	31	7 items
Iowa Tests of Basic Skills, Test A1: Arithmetic Concepts	10	14	4 items
Stanford Achievement Test, Form W, Intermediate II: Word Meaning	18	26	8 items

results in early September were poorer than those for the previous spring. For this example, the previous May mean (not shown) was 5.2. The real gain, then, for the year is 1.1 grade equivalents rather than the apparent 1.3. It would be inappropriate to pay the contractor for a mean gain of 1.3.

Another possible overpayment on the contract can result by holding final testing early and extrapolating the previous per-week growth to the weeks or months that follow. In Texarkana, as in most schools, spring progress was not as good as winter. If an accurate evaluation of contract instructional services is to be made, repeated testing, perhaps a month-by-month record of learning performances, needs to be considered.

Most performance contracts pay off on an individual student basis. The contractor may be paid for each student who gains more than an otherwise expected amount. This practice is commendable in that it emphasizes the importance of each individual learner and makes the contract easier to understand, but it bases payment on a precarious mark: the gain score.

Just how unreliable is the performance-test gain score? For a typical stan-

TABLE 3
Learning Calendar for a Typical Fifth-Grade Class.

	S	O	N	D	J	F	M	A	M
	|	|	|	|	|	|	|	|	|
Mean achievement score	5.0		5.3		5.6	5.9		6.2	6.3

dardized achievement test with two parallel forms. A and B, we might find the following characteristics reported in the test's technical manual:

Reliability of Test A = +.84.
Reliability of Test B = +.84.
Correlation of Test A with Test B = +.81.

Almost all standardized tests have reliability coefficients at this level. Using the standard formula,[9] one finds a disappointing level of reliability for the measurement of improvement:

Reliability gain scores (A–B or B–A) = +.16.

The test manual indicates the raw score and grade-equivalent standard deviations. For one widely used test, they are 9.5 items and 2.7 years, respectively. Using these values we can calculate the errors to be expected. *On the average,* a student's raw score would be in error by 2.5 items, grade equivalent would be in error by 0.72 year, and grade-equivalent *gain score* would be in error by 1.01 year. The error is indeed large.

Consider what this means for the not unusual contract whereby the student is graduated from the program, and the contractor is paid for his instruction, on any occasion that his performance score rises above a set value. Suppose— with the figures above—the student exits when his improvement is one grade equivalent or more. Suppose also, to make this situation simpler, that there is *no* intervening training and that the student is not influenced by previous testing. Here are three ways of looking at the same situation:

> Suppose that a contract student takes a different parallel form of the criterion test on three successive days immediately following the pretest. The chances are better than fifty-fifty than on *one* of these tests the student will gain a year or more in performance and appear to be ready to graduate from the program.
>
> Suppose that three students are tested with a parallel form immediately after the pretest. The chances are better than fifty-fifty that one of the three students—entirely due to errors of measurement—will gain a year or more and appear ready to graduate.
>
> Suppose that one hundred students are admitted to contract instruction and pretested. After a period of time involving no training, they are tested again, and the students gaining a year are graduated. After another period of time, another test and another graduation. After the fourth terminal testing, even though no instruction has occurred, the chances are better than fifty-fifty that two-thirds of the students will be graduated.

[9]Robert L. Thorndike and Elizabeth Hagen, *Measurement and Evaluation in Psychology and Education,* 3rd ed. (New York: John Wiley & Sons, 1969), p. 197.

In other words, owing to unreliability, gain scores can appear to reflect learning that actually does not occur.

The unreliability will give an equal number of false impressions of deteriorating performance. These errors (false gains and false losses) will balance out for a large group of students. If penalities for losses are paid by the contractor at the rate bonuses are paid for gains, the contractor will not be overpaid. But according to the way contracts are being written, typified in the examples above, the error in the gain scores does not balance out; it works in favor of the contractor. Measurement errors could be capitalized upon by unscrupulous promoters. Appropriate checks against these errors are built into the better contracts.

Errors in individual gain scores can be reduced by using longer tests. A better way to indicate true gain is to calculate the discrepancy between actual and expected final performances. Expectations can be based on the group as a whole or on an outside control group. Another way is to write the contract on the basis of mean scores for the group of students. (This would have the increased advantage of discouraging the contractor from giving perferential treatment within the project to students who are in a position to make high payoff gains.) Corrections for the unreliability of gain scores are possible, but they are not likely to be considered if the educators and contractors are statistically naive.

Probably the source of the greatest misinterpretation of the effects of remedial instruction is regression effects. Regression effects are easily overlooked but need not be; they are correctable. For any pretest score, the expected regression effect can be calculated. Regression effects make the poorest scorers look better the next time tested. Whether measurements are error-laden or error-free, meaningful or meaningless, when there is differential change between one measurement occasion and another (when there is less-than-perfect correlation), the lowest original scorers will make the greatest gains and the highest original scorers will make the least. On the average, posttest scores will, relative to their corresponding pretest scores, lie in the direction of the mean. This is the regression effect. Lord discussed this universal phenomenon and various ways to correct for it.[10]

The demand for performance contracts has occurred where conventional instructional programs fail to develop—for a sizable number of students—minimum competence in basic skills. Given a distribution of skill test scores, the lowest-scoring students—the ones most needing assistance—are identified. It is reasonable to suppose that under unchanged instructional programs they would drop even farther behind the high-scoring students. If a retest is given,

[10]Frederick M. Lord, "Elementary Models of Measuring Change," in *Problems in Measuring Change*, Chaster W. Harris, (ed.) (Madison. Wis.: University of Wisconsin Press, 1963), pp. 21–38.

however, after any period of instruction (conventional or special) or of no instruction, these students will no longer be the poorest performers. Some of them will be replaced by others who appear to be most in need of special instruction. Instruction is not the obvious influence here—regression is. The regression effect is not due to test unreliability, but it causes some of the same misinterpretations. The contract should read that instruction will be reimbursed when gain exceeds that attributable to regression effects. The preferred evaluation design would call for control group(s) of similar students to provide a good estimate of the progress the contract students would have made in the absence of the special instruction.

The Social Process

The hazards of specific performance testing and performance contracting are more than curricular and psychometric. Social and humanistic challenges should be raised, too. The teacher has a special opportunity and obligation to observe the influence of testing on social behavior.

Performance contracting has the unique ability to put the student in a position of administrative influence. He can make the instruction appear better or worse than it actually is by his performance on tests. Even if he is quite young, the student will know that his good work will benefit the contractor. Sooner or later he is going to know that, if he tests poorly at the beginning, he can benefit himself and the contractor through his later achievement. Bad performances are in his repertoire, and he may be more anxious to make the contractor look bad than to make himself look good. Or he may be under undue pressure to do well on the posttests. These are pupil-teacher interactions that should be watched carefully. More responsibility for school control possibly should accrue to students, but performance contracts seem a devious way to give it.

To motivate the student to learn and to make him want more contract instruction, many contractors use material or opportunity-to-play rewards. (Dorsett used such merchandise as transistor radios.) Other behavior modification strategies are common. The proponents of such strategies argue that, once behavior has been oriented to appropriate tasks, the students can gradually be shifted from extrinsic rewards to intrinsic. That they *can* be shifted is probably true; that it will happen without careful, deliberate work by the instruction staff is unlikely. It is not difficult to imagine a performance-contract situation in which the students become even less responsive to the rewards of conventional instruction.

In mid-1971, performance contracting appears to be popular with the current administration in Washington because it encourages private businesses to participate in a traditionally public responsibility. It is popular among some school administrators because if affords new access to federal funds, because it is a way to get new talent working on old problems, and because the administrator can easily blame the outside agency and the government if the contract instruction is unsuccessful. It is unpopular with the American Federation of Teachers because it reduces the control the union has over school operations, and it reduces the teacher's role as a chooser of what learning students need most. Performance contracting is popular among most instructional technologists because it is based on well-researched principles of teaching and because it enhances their role in school operations.

The accountability movement as a whole is likely to be a success or failure on such sociopolitical items. The measurement of the performance of performance contracting is an even more hazardous procedure than the measurement of student performances.

Summary

Without yielding to the temptation to undercut new efforts to provide instruction, educators should continue to be apprehensive about evaluating teaching on the basis of performance testing alone. They should know how difficult it is to represent educational goals with statements of objectives and how costly it is to provide suitable criterion testing. They should know that the common-sense interpretation of these results is frequently wrong. Still, many members of the profession think that evaluation controls are extravagant and mystical.

Performance contracting has emerged because people inside and outside the schools are dissatisfied with the instruction some children are getting. Implicit in the contracts is the expectation that available tests can measure the newly promised learning. The standardized test alone cannot measure the specific outcomes of an individual student with sufficient precision.

Extending the Boundaries of Accountability

Accountability and other reform efforts are aimed at improving the educational process. As we focus our attention on accountability, we must not forget that there are other reform efforts gaining in popularity and strengthening the trend toward educational change and innovation. The role of accountability within this wider trend is considered in this closing section.

Both Mario D. Fantini and Don Davies argue that the public has lost confidence in the schools. To head off a possible collision between educators and the public, they believe that professionals should be held responsible for their work and that a greater variety of educational opportunities should be made available. Fantini proposes an "internal voucher" plan that would permit teachers, students, and parents to develop programs within the school that meet what they themselves feel are their particular needs. In the final article, Davies discusses the new consumer sophistication and its effects on education. He also considers what impact the new education renewal sites and teacher centers will have on the public schools.

Needed: Radical Reform of Schools To Make Accountability Work

Mario D. Fantini

No matter how you look at it, the current push for accountability cannot be met by our present structure of public education. The structure handicaps the ability of the professional educator to be responsive to public demands, except in conventional ways that will receive even more public resistance.

Especially threatened by the push for accountability are the "front-line" agents of schools, teachers and principals. Right now they see themselves on a collision course with the public, a fact that has sent them running to their professional organizations for protection.

Given the nature of the major public demands for accountability, it is not surprising that teachers and other school agents feel they need protection. The demands, which fall into at least four interrelated categories, are formidable:

1. *Fiscal matters*. Faced with an inflationary economy and spiraling property taxes, overtaxed citizens have rebelled against school costs. They are "watching" the school budget much more closely and even are raising questions about specific line items. In the process, they are questioning accepted norms especially meaningful to teachers—like automatic salary increments.

2. *Educational productivity*. Citizens want to know if they're getting the most for their educational dollar and if a relationship between school programs and educational objectives exists. They have begun to blame the school and teachers for Johnny's failure to read, his lack of motivation, his negative attitudes toward school, his dislike of certain programs. In short, they are questioning the schools' leadership patterns, instructional procedures, and institutional arrangements.

3. *Consumer participation in educational decision-making*. There is a growing sense that teachers, principals, and administrators control education through decision making that favors professional interests rather than the interests of students and their parents. The public has the impression that educators are accountable to no one but themselves. This

Dr. Fantini is Dean of Education at the State University of New York (New Paltz). This article originally appeared in *Nation's Schools* (May 1972). © Copyright 1972 by McGraw-Hill, Inc. It was taken from Mario D. Fantini, *Public Schools of Choice: Alternatives in Education* (New York: Simon & Schuster, 1973). Reprinted by permission.

is leading certain citizens to demand a new governance system for education, one in which the community is closely connected with the internal affairs of the public schools.

Because they have been withdrawn from internal school matters for for so long, these citizens often lack the information and experience to make their call for accountability realistic. At times they tend to make simplistic demands on teachers—"You are paid to teach." "I want my child at grade level." "I'm holding you personally accountable." Such syllogisms are simplistic because they ignore the fact that professional talent can be thwarted by an institutionalized system, and because teaching and learning are influenced by many factors beyond the control of the teacher.

4. *Consumer satisfaction.* While related to the growing loss of confidence in public schools, consumer satisfaction extends also to the problem of providing quality education to a *diverse* consumer population. Over the years diversity has become a value which large numbers of citizens want to preserve and cultivate by connecting the school program with the particular learner, his style, and his cultural group. Put an end to the common learning and common educational process found in most schools, they say.

In line with this demand, many educational consumers are raising questions about the psycho-social effects of schooling—what the school as a social system is, or is not, doing to children. Parents are expressing dissatisfaction with teacher attitudes, for example, and with how certain teachers relate to children. They are concerned that their children might be exposed to teachers who may be psychologically damaging. They want teachers sensitive to cultural identity.

These four dimensions of accountability impose on the educator enormous responsibilities which he cannot discharge unless fundamental reform of American education takes place. Said somewhat differently, if a teacher, principal or administrator attempts to deal with the new wave of accountability by attempting to improve the institution rather than reform it, a major collision between professionals and the public will be unavoidable. Its effect will be devastating on the aspirations of society.

American educators find themselves inside a public institution forged during the nineteenth century. Educators have spent enormous time and energy trying to make this nineteenth-century model of education work for twentieth-century needs. They have developed an elaborate professional establishment in a genuine attempt to improve the institution. Various professional organizations have been established to strengthen professional standards, and numerous professional meetings have been conducted to develop continuing awareness for encouraging new effectiveness in learning.

Through these and other accomplishments, educators have helped public schools respond to public demands for such programs as special education, adult education, vocational education, early childhood education, and compensatory education for the economically disadvantaged. But while the public school has been responsive, it has become so by adding on layers to a basic structure forged at another time. The add-on strategy for trying to respond to the demands of society now can take us no farther, for the new accountability is in terms of the basic structure of education and its inability to deal with the continual demands for quality education from a pluralistic consumer population.

Subjected to economic distress, a society more diverse than ever before is demanding increased levels of quality education and is unwilling and unable to pay as it has in the past. Realizing the critical importance of education to their survival, more parents and students join the protest, placing more pressure on the schools and schoolmen. Professionals, in turn, become defensive and seek greater protection from their professional organizations.

Public pressure reaches the policymakers in state legislatures, who begin to consider new budget restrictions for public education and to experiment with such proposals as performance contracting or educational vouchers. These plans bring additional resistance and resentment from educators, literally forcing them to consolidate further (*e.g.* NEA and AFT).

If public schools are to stop running counter to current public demands, they and their agents must *stop*: (1) responding to a pluralistic consumer group by trying to improve the standard school program so that it will work for everyone; (2) developing a more-of-the-same stance *vis-à-vis* educational improvement, adding on more staff to upgrade whatever aspect of the school program isn't working at the moment; (3) developing internal political dynamics in which teachers, long considered the doormats of the system, form very powerful teacher organizations to get better salaries and working conditions and to protect their interests and rights.

Teachers especially are constrained by the structure of schools. Not having been prepared to teach for cultural pluralism or to deal with the wide range of different learning styles that converge in the classroom, teachers attempt to survive. They learn to teach on the job, developing their own teaching style in the process. Many find it natural simply to impose their learning style on a group of youngsters and to blame the youngsters who do not respond for failure.

In this sort of situation, if the principal attempts to move the student from one room to another, severe internal problems often result. The teacher might accuse the principal of siding with the student and might report the episode to his teacher organization. The principal then might become suspect and have difficulty gaining staff cooperation. Because teachers are more powerful politically than students or principals, many students are forced into situations not conducive to growth and development.

Moreover, contractual protections won for teachers by their unions tend to freeze the teacher into an acceptable mold of operation. Salaries, hours of work, kinds of work, class size, and tenure become the standards by which quality education is measured. They all make sense if the mission is to make a uniform pattern of education better, but they may have little to do with real reform of public schools or with the range of complex demands emanating from diverse consumers.

Obviously, it is difficult to hold teachers accountable as individuals. How can the public hold teachers accountable? They are like individual players on an orchestra or football team. It is the total effort that counts. Although the school is the basic unit of accountability, teachers collectively have much of the power to generate reform. They must take the lead in establishing new relationships between themselves and parents. They must work cooperatively with administrators and principals to plan alternative approaches to current school programs.

The point is this: Our present institutional arrangements govern our professional behavior. We have developed operational norms that may make good sense inside the schools but not outside. We want to be responsive to the various public demands but find that we can respond only in ways that are unacceptable to the public. We cannot continue to go on this way.

When parents ask for increased individual attention for children, we must have a better response than "give us more money to lower class size." When people from poor communities complain that we are not educating their children, we must have a better response than compensatory education.

The task is not easy, to be sure. Adding to the difficulties are current public school arrangements that restrict the talents of teachers who want to move in new directions. Those who express interest in new forms of education, such as open classrooms or schools without walls, come directly into conflict with established norms.

Moreover, any reform proposal that questions established norms is immediately suspect in terms of vested interests and becomes the object of widespread professional criticism. We have witnessed this reaction to virtually every major reform proposal—desegregation, decentralization, vouchers, performance contracting.

It is vitally important for us to understand that these behaviors are quite reasonable and proper given the present framework of public education. The environment of the public schools allows no other response.

Teachers are often right when they exclaim, "Parents don't understand our problems." Well, how can they? Parents do not "live" inside the school as do teachers. We cannot expect parents and other citizens to know what they have not experienced.

The fundamental concern, of course, is that the accountability drama unfolding among teachers, parents and students is likely to culminate in a "we-they" type of political confrontation. If teachers, trapped by the same system that restricts the consumer, cannot break out of the cycle, the confrontation is certain to come.

Is there any way of dealing with the dilemma? We certainly have learned some lessons to help us. The trick will be to make any reform proposal live up to these lessons. Reform proposals must be realistic; they must confront the current forces in schools, including internal political realities. Time is running out. Now is not the time to blast the public schools for being in a crisis. It is time to offer corrective proposals aimed at reforming one of our most basic social institutions.

In this spirit, we propose our plan: Public Schools of Choice. This plan is based upon a type of internal voucher, reflecting more of a change in perception and philosophy than anything else. These seven criteria served as ground rules in formulating the plan. This plan

1. Demonstrates adherence to a comprehensive set of educational objectives—not particular ones. Proposals cannot, for example, emphasize only emotional growth at the expense of intellectual development. The converse is also true. Comprehensive educational objectives deal with work careers, citizenship, talent development, intellectual and emotional growth, problem solving, critical thinking, and the like.

2. Does not substantially increase per-student expenditure over that of established programs. To advance an idea that doubles or triples the budget will be best place the proposal in the ideal, but not practical, category. An important factor for reformers to bear in mind is that the new arena will deal with wiser use of old money, not the quest for new funds.

3. Does not advocate any form of exclusivity—racial, religious, or economic. Solutions cannot deny equal access to any particular individual or group.

4. Is not superimposed. The days of a small group planning for or doing to others are fading away.

5. Respects the rights of all concerned parties and must apply to everyone. It cannot appear to serve the interests of one group only. Thus, for instance, if decentralization plans of urban school systems are interpreted to serve only minority communities, then the majority community may very well oppose such efforts. Similarly, if plans appear to favor professionals, then the community may be in opposition.

6. Does not propose a single across-the-board solution. Attempts at uniform solutions are almost never successful.
7. Advocates a process of change that is democratic and maximizes individual decision making. Participation by the individual in the decisions that affect his life is vital to assure widespread support.

The problem with most American public education is that it is a monolithic means for achieving a common set of educational ends. That is to say, the public schools offer a rather uniform educational diet to its diverse consumers. Its single set of teaching goods and techniques handicaps many students and teachers.

Historically, those who could afford it had the option of sending their children to alternative schools, usually in the private sectors. Why cannot public schools develop alternative forms of education within their own framework? Why cannot teachers whose teaching styles differ be allowed to develop alternative forms of instruction? Why cannot those students and parents who prefer an option developed by a teacher select it by choice? Those teachers, students, and parents who prefer the standard process have a right to it. Those teachers, students, and parents who prefer alternative methods should also have this right.

The plan we propose can be implemented in any school, at any grade level, almost immediately. For example, if a school has four first grade classes, three could be traditional and one open. All that is required is that one of the four first grade teachers possess the teaching style, disposition, and willingness to offer an optional "open classroom." Meetings with parents could be held to provide basic information on the open classroom. Those parents who wished to explore this matter further could meet again with the interested teacher and administration. After a series of such sessions, it is entirely possible that parents, students, and teachers will choose another kind of option. Individualization would occur by matching teacher-style, learning environment, and learner style.

At the high school level, some teachers and students may favor an alternative "school within a school" or "mini-school" based on the principle of multicultural education. In Philadelphia, an alternative public school was established based on the "school without walls" concept, in which the city itself became the classroom. This school without walls (Parkway Program) was not imposed on any teachers, students, or parents. Rather, all parties involved in the program joined by choice.

A school or school system could develop a range of educational options:

1. *Traditional.* The school is graded and emphasizes the students' acquisition of basic skills (i.e., reading, writing, mathematics) by cognitive methods. The basic learning unit is the classroom, manned by one or more teachers who

direct and instruct students in their tasks. Students are encouraged to adapt to the style of the school. Youngsters with diagnosed learning handicaps participate in remedial programs. The educational and fiscal policy of this school is determined entirely by a central board of education.

2. *Open and Non-graded.* This school resembles the primary schools and Leicestershire Infant Schools of Britain. The "school" is divided into learning areas, each containing many constructional and manipulative materials. Youngsters work individually or in small groups on various specialized learning projects, with the teachers acting as facilitators, rather than managers. Many activities occur outside the school building.

3. *Career-oriented.* This school fosters learning by experience. The school is responsible for identifying individual talent and prescribing suitable experiences for its nourishment. Various learning and teaching styles are operational here, and concrete performance is deemed as important as theoretical proficiency. This program is geared toward the work world.

4. *Automated.* The programs at this kind of school utilize technological devices. Computers are used for diagnosis of students' needs and abilities. The library contains banks of tape recordings and "talking," "listening," and manipulative carrels that can be student-operated. Closed-circuit television is offered as well as Nova-type retrieval systems for student-teacher conferences on individual learning problems.

5. *Total Community School.* This school operates on a 12 to 14 hour basis for at least six days a week all year round. Adults and children participate in educational and civic programs. The facility provides services for health, legal aid, and employment. Paraprofessionals or community teachers assist in every phase of the regular school program, and the school is controlled by a board of community representatives. This board hires the two chief administrators, one of whom directs all other activities in the school. More than a school, this institution is a community center.

6. *Montessori.* Students move at their own pace and are largely self-directed. The learning areas are rich with creative selection. The teacher functions within a specifically defined methodology, but she is a guide, not a director. The development of sensory perception is emphasized in Montessori classrooms.

7. *Multi-culture School.* Named for the model in San Francisco, this school is marked by its ethnic heterogeneity. As many as five ethnic groups may be equally represented, and for part of each day the groups are separated for homogeneous learning. Classes are concerned with the language, customs, history, and heritage of the respective group. Several times a week one group shares an aspect of its culture with the other students Diversity is the outstanding value here, and the curriculum is humanistic in content. Questions of group identity, inter-group identity, power, and individual identity are dis-

cussed. The school is governed by a policy board composed of equal numbers of parents and teachers that is only tangentially responsible to the central board of education.

8. *Performance Contract School.* Educational consumers subcontract with an educational firm to operate one of its public schools. In Gary, Indiana, Behavioral Research Laboratories is operating the Banneker Elementary School. Its contract with the public schools contains a money-back guarantee that the children in the school will achieve a certain set of educational objectives, such as reading at grade level. The Banneker program makes wide use of individualized reading materials developed by the company.

What we are suggesting here is an "internal voucher" system, i.e., educational alternatives within the framework of public education. Such a plan would, we believe, receive internal professional support and start to meet the numerous consumer demands.

These proposals, we believe, would strengthen the concept of public education in the United States, not weaken or destroy it. As a kind of supply and demand model, the internal voucher would stimulate development by conscientiously offering new and better ways of educating children without scrapping the best of the old. Certainly the plan could help relieve the strain on the overloaded standard public school process, while still including it as one of the legitimate alternatives to which a pluralistic consumer group is entitled.

Public schools have the manpower and the mechanism to develop an internal voucher framework immediately. At present, manpower is employed in trying to improve the one standard alternative—not in developing alternatives. This is why present proposals for the external voucher system favor private schools. Public schools, because of their monolithic nature, are viewed merely as *one* alternative.

Access to parent and community education and involvement is enhanced in a public schools of choice system. However, unless basic information about alternatives reaches students and parents, it will be difficult for an internal voucher plan to succeed.

It will be literally impossible to respond to the current demands for accountability by holding fast to a system of education that was forged in another century. This inability to be responsive can only result in a confrontation between the public and professionals.

The new emphasis on accountability provides the professional educator with an opportunity to build, at the request of the public, a new framework for public education without tearing down what has been developed thus far. Public Schools of Choice, or internal vouchers, would permit every teacher, every student, and every parent to exercise choice among education options inside the framework of public schools. This approach need not cost more money, but it does call for a different utilization of existing resources.

Toward a New Consumerism

Don Davies

Over the past decade, Americans have developed a new and continually increasing awareness of their roles as consumers. This awareness has made itself felt in the nation's corporate boardrooms and legislative chambers. Concepts such as "truth-in-packaging" and "truth-in-lending," that until recently were considered visionary, are today the law of the land. Consumers, in short, have demanded that industry assume increased responsibility for the quality of its products, and industry is beginning to meet that responsibility.

We in education, however, have only recently begun to feel the pressure of this new consumerism. We have had our crises and our challenges in the past and we have responded to them, but we have not been held truly accountable for the thousands of children for whom the road to failure began in kindergarten. In fact, education is probably the only area of our free-enterprise system in which the consumer rather than the producer is held responsible for the quality of the product.

As far as educators are concerned, the term *accountability* can be interpreted in several ways. There is accountability to the taxpayer, since, contrary to the standard American oversimplification, our free public schools are not free. They are paid for with tax money, and the taxpayer has a right to know what he is getting for his money. There is accountability to the Congress and to state and local legislative bodies. They are responsible for appropriating funds for educational programs and they have a right to know how productive these programs have been. But there is another type of accountability, the kind that holds teachers and aides and principals and superintendents and school board members accountable for the educational achievements of all of their clients—those who come to school well prepared to take advantage of its benefits as well as those who do not.

This concept of accountability calls for a revamping of much of the thinking about the roles of school personnel and educational institutions at all levels. It links student performance with teacher performance. It involves precisely stated educational goals and it forecasts achievement. It means, in effect, that schools and colleges will be judged on how they perform, rather than on what they promise; accountability places the burden of performance on the classroom teacher and school administrator alike.

Dr. Davies is Deputy Commissioner for Renewal, U.S. Office of Education.

To realize this kind of responsive and responsible educational system, people's attitudes must be changed. This applies not only to the people who run the schools, but also to those who run the institutions that control education—the colleges and universities, state departments of education, local education agencies, and the federal agencies responsible for developing education programs. There is a need for people and institutions capable of continuous change, continuous renewal, and continuous responsiveness to the changing needs of children and communities. Once there is an understanding of accountability, we can develop a powerful tool for effecting the kinds of reform and renewal that will produce a more responsible and more humane brand of education.

There are several attitudes that must be changed before the concept of accountability can become meaningful. One is the idea that labeling, sorting, and classifying children is the central task of the school. This attitude is held not only by educators, but by the general public as well. It is buttressed by a heavy emphasis on tests, bell-shaped curves, norms, ability grouping, and whatever else can be devised to guarantee that some children rank high and others low. This sorting-weeding-grouping concept that prevades the entire educational establishment from kindergarten to graduate school is designed to indicate beyond doubt who is destined for success and who for failure.

If this classifying of students were the chief task of the school, we could be satisfied that we have been diligent and enterprising in perfecting measurement instruments that do their job well. But schools are in business for another purpose. Their first job, whether at the kindergarten or graduate school level, is to develop human potential. The goal of education should not be to separate the successes from the failures, but to help each child find his own path to success. The consumers of education should demand this of us, and hold us accountable if we do not succeed.

Another attitude that relates to accountability concerns the tendency of school personnel—everyone from teachers and support personnel to administrators and school board members—to blame the failure of minority-group children from low-income families on anything but the eductors' incompetence.

They put the blame for his failure on the child himself, on his parents, on his home environment, on his appearance, or perhaps even on the suspicion that he does not bathe regularly. The sad fact is that in spite of all of the rhetoric about equalizing educational opportunity, we have not yet achieved equality of expectation. The evidence is very strong that it is difficult, perhaps even impossible, for these children to overcome the damaging impact of these negative attitudes and low expectations. Along with introducing the concept of accountability into the American educational system, we must put an end to making these educational alibis and inflicting this psychological damage on these children. If we do not, teachers will continue to teach ineffectively and their continued failure will cause their pupils to fail.

Many educators are also tied into an academic approach that stresses "input" rather than "output." This means, for example, that teaching is evaluated by the style and organization of a lecture, rather than by what the students can do or have learned as a result of listening to the lecture. A classroom is judged on its brightness, orderliness, and quietness, rather than on the behavior and skills that the children develop as a result of being in that classroom. In approaching the training of teachers, educators stress the need for the completion of a certain number of education courses and the acquisition of a certain number of credits, rather than the ability to teach. On those rare occasions when we do assess output, the tendency is to confine that evaluation to those outcomes that are easily measured—reading and math levels, particularly. These are areas in which we have already developed some reliable measuring instruments.

It would be a tragic distortion of the school's role if we failed to extend testing to other measures of student development. Positive attitudes toward oneself and others, respect for the culture and values of others, and a willingness and ability to participate in the processes of organizations, institutions, and government are all qualities that can be nurtured in the classroom. A school's success or failure in this regard can be measured, not by standardized tests, but by examining a pupil's attendance record, tardiness record, and his willingness to cooperate efforts with other students and teachers. The ultimate measure is the student's decision to stay in school or drop out. Furthermore, attitudes can be measured through observation. It is possible to observe enthusiasm, boredom, excitement, and alert interest, and these kinds of subjective tests are every bit as conclusive and informative as those tests developed by national testing services.

Having outlined the attitudinal changes necessary for a workable system of accountability, we must now examine the ways in which this concept can be applied. Basically, accountability is a participatory process through which the schools and community can judge what schools can and should do, decide what conditions and resources are needed to function effectively, and determine whether or not their objectives have been achieved.

A participatory process requires that students, teachers, administrators, parents, and others in the community be genuinely involved in examining needs, determining goals, and evaluating results. It requires the involvement and participation of the school board, teachers' organizations, and parent, community, and student groups. Finally, a participatory process necessitates that decisions affecting how the accountability process is put into effect and how it operates be determined by the individual school and community, and not by some predetermined national standards.

The U.S. Office of Education (USOE) has attempted to stimulate educational renewal by helping schools learn to develop programs tailored to their specific requirements. This effort represents a comprehensive, unified attack on major educational problems. It concentrates on individual schools and clusters of schools, and encourages the kind of overall participation that is the key to a successful system of accountability.

The USOE is consolidating under the Office of the Deputy Commissioner for Renewal most of the previously scattered discretionary programs. Concentrating funds in this way enables a limited number of school systems to install totally new programs involving all aspects of the school system, and eliminates the need for schools to submit separate applications for funding under each program.

Assuming there is appropriate funding, this renewal effort involves approximately two hundred "renewal sites," half of which are planning their programs and the rest in operation. Each site consists of approximately ten schools, and each is located in areas with large concentrations of disadvantaged children.

Rather than telling the schools what USOE thinks they need, USOE asks the schools to describe their problems and suggest their own solutions. This assessment is made by local school officials working together with teachers, students, parents, and residents of each renewal neighborhood. These groups are encouraged to consider solutions based on the products of educational research and development that too often in the past have failed to reach the classroom.

For the first time, USOE is asking communities to say what they need, and apart from requiring that the programs meet various legal criteria, USOE will consider any plan that makes sound educational sense and represents significant change. There are three important requirements: (1) the proposal must show evidence of state and local commitment, such as a willingness to increase or at least maintain current levels of spending in the renewal schools; (2) the proposal must be comprehensive, involving all aspects of the school, its staff and clientele; and (3) objectives must be stated in precise, measurable terms, such as raising average student achievement by a definite percentage over that to be expected in a normal school year or decreasing the gap in achievement between disadvantaged and middle-class students in the same district by a stated percentage.

Presuming that a community's assessment of its needs and its proposed solutions are in line with these broad requirements, the proposal, no matter how many components it includes, can be submitted in a single application. Proposals relating to research, teacher training, paraprofessional aides, audiovisual materials, and medical and dental examinations, for instance, can all be lumped together in one document.

The fundamental implementation mechanism of the USOE program, apart from the schools themselves, are teacher centers, located at each renewal site and serving all schools involved in the project. These centers can further educational reform by helping to change the attitudes and improve the competence and skill of the people staffing the schools. In essence, the centers act as middlemen between the schools and such educational resources as the USOE, colleges and universities, civic and educational associations, private industry, and private citizens who can help make the renewal strategy successful.

The renewal strategy also provides for the establishment of a corps of educational extension agents, most of whom operate out of state departments of education. They are able to link the professionals in the schools to federal, state, and local researchers in a potentially productive partnership. This program, a key feature of the renewal strategy, is modeled after the very successful agricultural extension system whose agents keep farmers informed of progress in agricultural research and development. These educational extension agents will not come to the schools to tell teachers what to do, but rather to ask them what help they need, what kinds of ideas they want to explore, and to inform them of federal resources that they might not know about.

Information from the agents is useful in determining what resources are available to help solve a particular problem and in assessing how the experience could tie in with the USOE's tasks in research and development. In short, this program represents a new determination within the USOE to get the new products of educational research into the hands of the classroom teachers.

The final component of this renewal strategy is evaluation. We want to know what worked, what did not work, and—to the degree we are able to determine—the reasons for failure and success. The USOE will not simply judge a program good or bad and then close the books on it. The great majority of renewal projects will be financed for approximately five years and the USOE plans to work with the project directors during that time to iron out problems, and even, if shown necessary, to alter the plans. In short, the intent of the renewal strategy is to make innovation a way of life in education by providing a change mechanism that enables a school staff to alter instructional practices not just once, but as often as changing circumstances dictate. The strategy is designed to help the staff of a school think through its own problems rather than accepting remedies offered by outside agencies, and help them persevere through the disappointments inevitable in any effort to promote change.

This renewal strategy is an expression of faith in the people who are now running our schools, and a recognition of the need to solicit their views on how they would conduct their jobs if they had the freedom and resources to do as they wished. This renewal strategy, moreover, provides the foundation for a consumer-oriented system of education based on a just and workable concept of teacher accountability. It offers a mechanism for revamping the roles of educational personnel and institutions by providing them with the resources and the encouragement to respond to individual needs of individual students.

This renewal strategy should do much to improve the quality of the educational product, but we must remember that it provides only a partial solution to the problem. Before we can hope to provide all students humane and individualized educational experiences, we must bring about some changes in our teacher-training institutions. If the accountability concept is to be completely workable, it must be introduced into the colleges and universities that prepare educational personnel. Too many of these institutions rely on the reward and punishment system in training their teachers; and their graduates, in turn, use reward and punishment as tools in their own teaching. The schools sort and weed and classify teacher candidates just as their alumni sort and weed and classify their students in the classroom. They evaluate by written tests rather than by performance, and if the graduated teacher turns out to be incompetent, they do not attribute this result to incompetent teachers of teachers.

Unfortunately, much of education is transmitting only one part of culture and civilization—the factual part. As schools concentrate on cognitive learning, they fail to discover the feelings, wishes, needs, and concerns of the students. The whole concept of the affective approach is neglected. Until teacher-training institutions revise their attitudes and curricula relating to affective learning, they will continue to produce teachers unable to relate with pupils as human beings.

In recent years, the USOE has concentrated a great deal on bringing about reform in teacher education. One approach has been to aid school districts that take the position that they have a role to play in staff development. The USOE is underwriting programs that provide leverage for school systems negotiating with colleges and universities for changes affecting not only those being trained but the trainers as well. It is proceeding on the premise that the training of teachers cannot be left solely to either the colleges or the schools of education. This approach offers opportunities for local school districts to share in the responsibility for preparing recruits, and the USOE wants to encourage this growing partnership between schools and colleges. By encouraging work-study arrangements and internship programs, the USOE sees opportunities to plow back into the training programs much of what the trainees learn during their work experiences. By joining the schools and colleges in a continuing working arrangement, we can eventually break down the meaningless barriers between pre-service and in-service training.

Another way to reform teacher education and prepare teachers who will be in a position to be held accountable is by encouraging performance- or competency-based teacher-training programs, with certification procedures based on the same criteria. School personnel, trained under these programs and certified because of proven competency, are likely to be equipped to be held accountable for their pupils' learning. The same cannot be said of personnel qualified to teach solely by their ability to pass a prescribed number of courses.

How can teacher-education institutions be held accountable for the quality of their graduates? One way is to base accreditation of these institutions on the performance of their graduates in the classroom. School districts might also adopt the policy of hiring new teachers only from institutions that are willing to be held accountable for the performance of their alumni. Until very recently, such proposals might have been scoffed at. But this is a buyer's market. The general teacher shortage is over. Colleges and universities are now turning out more teachers than are needed and school systems are in a position to be selective about the personnel they employ.

So this whole concept of accountability, with all that it implies for the improvement of education at all levels, is a very practical notion. Truth in packaging for the consumers of education is an idea whose time has come.